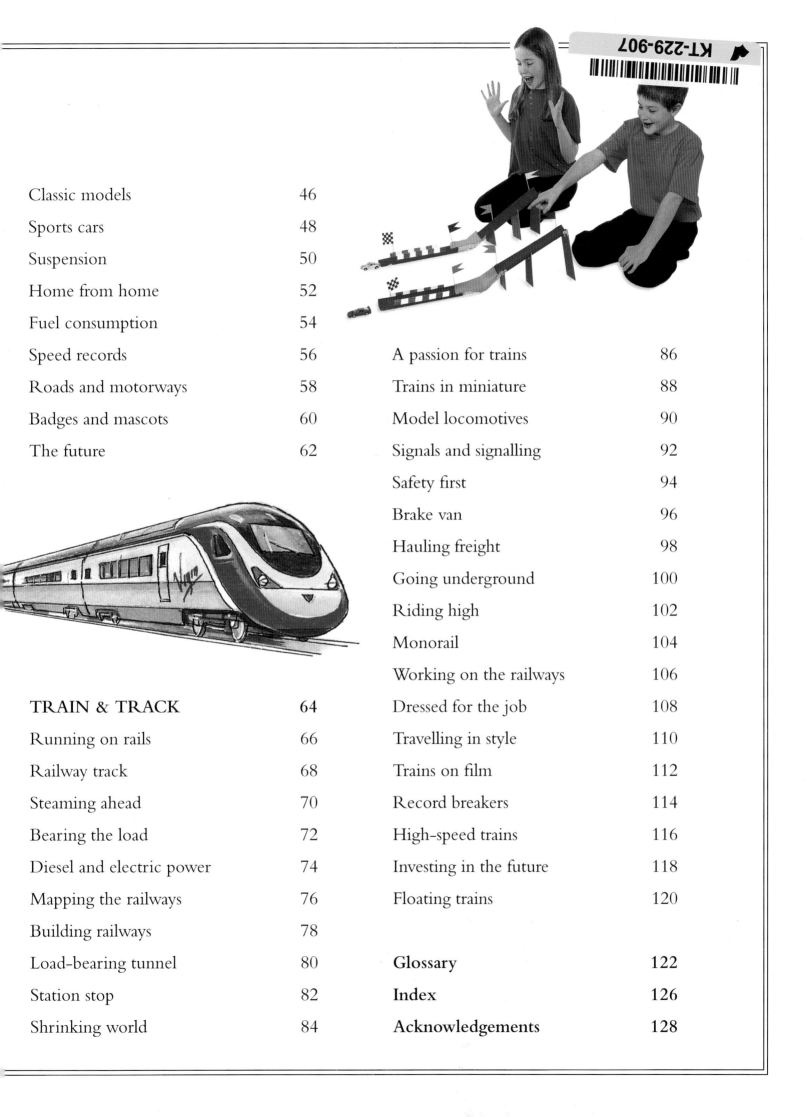

INTRODUCTION

THE HISTORY of the modern world is closely interwoven with the history of machines that many people now use every day. The machines that move people from place to place are perhaps most important of all. Around the world, people rely on trains and cars to transport them quickly and safely to school, to work, on holiday and back again. Yet these machines, which we often take for granted, were not always around to make life easier.

Before the 19th century, travelling anywhere was extremely slow. Roads were often just muddy tracks on which horse-drawn coaches moved only a few miles an hour, and there were no railways at all. At the beginning of the 1800s the steam locomotive was invented in Great Britain.

Above: The invention of the internal combustion engine revolutionized the way millions of people travelled.
Below: Steam-powered locomotives were developed in the 1800s and soon led to the world's first passenger trains.

CAR & ROAD, & TRACK

Peter Harrison

CONSULTANTS Peter Cahill and Michael Harris

southwater

This edition is published by Southwater

Southwater is an imprint of Anness Publishing Ltd
Hermes House, 88-89 Blackfriars Road,
London SE1 8HA
tel. 020 7401 2077; fax 020 7633 9499
www.southwaterbooks.com; info@anness.com

© Anness Publishing Ltd 2004

UK agent: The Manning Partnership Ltd,
6 The Old Dairy, Melcombe Road,
Bath BA2 3LR; tel. 01225 478444;
fax 01225 478440; sales@manning-partnership.co.uk

UK distributor: Grantham Book Services Ltd,
Isaac Newton Way, Alma Park Industrial Estate,
Grantham, Lincs NG31 9SD; tel. 01476 541080;
fax 01476 541061; orders@gbs.tbs-ltd.co.uk

North American agent/distributor: National Book
Network, 4501 Forbes Boulevard, Suite 200, Lanham,
MD 20706; tel. 301 459 3366; fax 301 429 5746;
www.nbnbooks.com

Australian agent/distributor: Pan Macmillan Australia,
Level 18, St Martins Tower, 31 Market St, Sydney,
NSW 2000; tel. 1300 135 113; fax 1300 135 103;
customer.service@macmillan.com.au

New Zealand agent/distributor: David Bateman Ltd,
30 Tarndale Grove, Off Bush Road, Albany, Auckland;
tel. (09) 415 7664; fax (09) 415 8892

Publisher: Joanna Lorenz
Editorial Director: Judith Simons
Editor: Clare Gooden
Designers: Sarah Melrose and Caroline Reeves,
   Aztec Design
Photographer: John Freeman
Stylist: Melanie Williams
Picture Researcher: Gwen Campbell
Illustrator: Guy Smith
Production Controller:
   Lee Sargent

Previously published in two
separate volumes,
Investigations: Cars and
Investigations: Trains

10 9 8 7 6 5 4 3 2 1

CONTENTS

CAR & ROAD, TRAIN & TRACK

Peter Harrison

CONSULTANTS **Peter Cahill and Michael Harris**

southwater

This edition is published by Southwater

Southwater is an imprint of Anness Publishing Ltd
Hermes House, 88-89 Blackfriars Road,
London SE1 8HA
tel. 020 7401 2077; fax 020 7633 9499
www.southwaterbooks.com; info@anness.com

© Anness Publishing Ltd 2004

UK agent: The Manning Partnership Ltd,
6 The Old Dairy, Melcombe Road,
Bath BA2 3LR; tel. 01225 478444;
fax 01225 478440; sales@manning-partnership.co.uk

UK distributor: Grantham Book Services Ltd,
Isaac Newton Way, Alma Park Industrial Estate,
Grantham, Lincs NG31 9SD; tel. 01476 541080;
fax 01476 541061; orders@gbs.tbs-ltd.co.uk

North American agent/distributor: National Book
Network, 4501 Forbes Boulevard, Suite 200, Lanham,
MD 20706; tel. 301 459 3366; fax 301 429 5746;
www.nbnbooks.com

Australian agent/distributor: Pan Macmillan Australia,
Level 18, St Martins Tower, 31 Market St, Sydney,
NSW 2000; tel. 1300 135 113; fax 1300 135 103;
customer.service@macmillan.com.au

New Zealand agent/distributor: David Bateman Ltd,
30 Tarndale Grove, Off Bush Road, Albany, Auckland;
tel. (09) 415 7664; fax (09) 415 8892

Publisher: Joanna Lorenz
Editorial Director: Judith Simons
Editor: Clare Gooden
Designers: Sarah Melrose and Caroline Reeves,
   Aztec Design
Photographer: John Freeman
Stylist: Melanie Williams
Picture Researcher: Gwen Campbell
Illustrator: Guy Smith
Production Controller:
   Lee Sargent

Previously published in two
separate volumes,
Investigations: Cars and
Investigations: Trains

10 9 8 7 6 5 4 3 2 1

CONTENTS

Soon after, locomotives were used to pull carriages in which passengers sat, and the first railways were born. Afterwards, they were built all over the world.

The internal combustion engine that powers cars was not perfected until much later, at the end of the 19th century in Germany. Within decades cars were being built in their millions by Henry Ford in the USA. Now the sheer number of cars in many parts of the world has created a real problem. Cars create air pollution, which is damaging our environment, and the more cars there are, the more roads are needed, and these take up valuable space. However, increased environmental awareness means that cars are now being built that pollute the air less than earlier models.

Although cars are now an extremely popular form of transport, railways still play an important role. The modern railways in countries such as Japan and France are famous worldwide for their speed and efficiency, and provide a standard of service to which many other countries aspire.

Discover the past, present and future of transport, where the machines we use are being developed and improved all the time.

Above left: Sports cars like this Lamborghini Diablo travel very fast. Cars today can be a hobby and a status symbol as well as a means of travelling.
Above: The increasing number of cars around the world has led to the construction of many new roads, and this has raised environmental concerns.
Below: Modern railway companies are investing in the future with high-speed tilting trains, electric trains and even magnetic or floating trains.

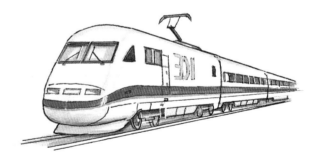

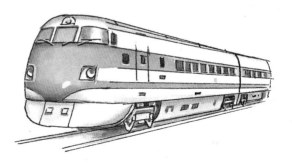

CAR & ROAD

THE JOURNEY BEGINS

CARS MAKE people mobile in a way that would have been impossible only a century ago. Then, a journey by road of just 50km could have taken an entire day. Nowadays, we can travel this distance in half an hour. The ability to go where you want, when you want, quickly, makes travelling much easier. Millions of people all over the world use cars to travel to work or to the shops, to go on holiday and to visit friends and relations. Horse-drawn carriages and carts, and walking, were the main forms of road transport for thousands of years before cars. Many roads were badly made. Because cars moved under their own power, and encouraged better road building, they allowed people to travel much more.

Hold on tight
Very early cars such as this Velo, made in Germany in 1893 by Karl Benz, had no covering bodywork. When Benz's daughter Clara went driving, she sat high above the road with very little to hang on to if the car hit a bump in the road.

By the numbers
The tachometer (rev. counter), speedometer and clock from a Rolls–Royce Silver Ghost have solid brass fittings and glass covers. They were assembled by hand. The instruments on early cars were often made by skilled craftworkers. The Silver Ghost was made continuously from 1906 until 1925.

Bold as brass
A gleaming brass horn and lamp are proud examples of the detailed work that went into making the first cars. Early cars were made with materials that would be far too expensive for most people nowadays. Seats were upholstered with thickly padded leather, because the cars had poor suspension and bumped a lot. This prevented the drivers and passengers from being jolted up and down too much.

Old bruiser

This Bentley was built before 1931, when the company was taken over by Rolls–Royce. Bentley built powerful and sturdy sports cars, some weighing up to 1700kg. They won many motor races in the 1920s and 1930s, such as the Le Mans 24-hour race in France. Big cars such as these were built on heavy metal chassis (frames). They had wood-framed bodies covered in metal and leather cloth, huge headlamps and large, wire-spoked wheels.

Egg on wheels

In the 1950s and 1960s, car makers began to make very small cars, such as this German BMW Isetta. Around 160,000 Isettas were produced between 1955 and 1962. Manufacturers developed small cars because they were cheaper to buy and to run, and used less parking space. The Isetta, like so many of the microcars, was powered by a small motorcycle engine.

Cool cruisin'

Cadillac was an American company known for its stylish designs. This Cadillac from the 1950s, with its large tail fins and shiny chrome, is a typical example. Many cars from the 1950s and 1960s, including this one, are known as classic cars. People like to collect them and restore them to their original condition.

Redhead

The Italian car maker Ferrari has a reputation for making very fast, very expensive cars. This 1985 Testarossa has a top speed of 290km/hour. Very few people can afford to own such a car. Even if they have the money, it takes great driving skill to get the best out of one.

Going nowhere?

The success of the car has its downside. Millions of people driving cars causes problems such as traffic jams and air pollution. Also, the building of new roads can spoil the countryside. These issues are being debated all over the world.

THE EARLIEST CARS

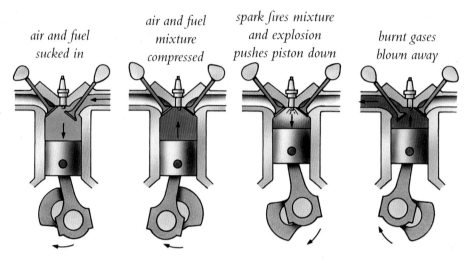

air and fuel sucked in

air and fuel mixture compressed

spark fires mixture and explosion pushes piston down

burnt gases blown away

AMONG THE most important builders of early cars and car engines were the Germans Nikolaus Otto, Karl Benz and Gottlieb Daimler. In the late 1800s, they built the first internal combustion engines using sprockets and chains to connect the engine to the wheels. Car engines are called internal (inside) combustion (burning) engines because they burn a mixture of fuel and air inside a small chamber. People had long been trying to find ways to make engines for road transport. In 1770, the Frenchman Nicholas-Joseph Cugnot made a steam engine that drove a three-wheeled cart. It was too heavy to use, however, and only two were built. The achievement of Benz, Otto and Daimler was to make a small engine that could produce enough power for road vehicles. The earliest cars are known as veteran (built before 1905) and Edwardian (built between 1905 and 1919). They were not as reliable as modern vehicles, but were sometimes more finely built.

Suck, squeeze, bang, blow

A car's piston (like an upturned metal cup) moves in a rhythm of four steps called the Otto cycle, after Nikolaus Otto. First, it moves down to suck in fuel mixed with air. Then it pushes up and compresses (squeezes) the mixture. The spark plug ignites the fuel. The bang of the explosion pushes the piston down again. When the piston moves up again, it blows out the burnt gases.

Trim trike

The three-wheeled Benz Motorwagen was first made in 1886. It was steered by a small hand lever on top of a tall steering column. Karl Benz began his career building carriages. He used this training when he built his first car in 1885. By 1888 Benz was employing 50 people to build his Motorwagens.

Follow my leader

Soon after the first cars were being driven on the roads, accidents started to happen. Until 1904, there was a law requiring a person carrying a red flag to walk in front of the car. This forced the car driver to go slowly. The flag was to warn people that a car was coming.

Remember this

Important military gentlemen pose for photos with their cars. They are not in the driving seats, however. They had chauffeurs to drive the cars for them. Car owners in the early 1900s liked to show their cars off. They often posed for photographs to keep for souvenirs.

Look out!

The car horns that early drivers sounded to warn pedestrians were very different from those in modern cars. When the driver squeezed the rubber bulb, air travelled through the tube and made a noise when it came out of the end.

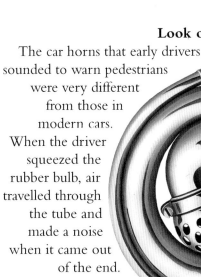

Bad weather

Early cars were hard to control at times because their braking and steering systems were not very effective. When bad weather such as snow made the ground slippery the car could easily run off the road. Even in modern cars with efficient brakes, and good tyres and steering, winter weather can make driving difficult.

All wrapped up

Drivers at the turn of the century wore thick goggles to protect their eyes, because their cars had no windscreen nor, indeed, any protective bodywork. The roads were not smooth and stones and dust were flung up by the wheels. Cold winds felt even colder in a moving, open car, so thick caps and heavy driving clothes were worn to keep warm.

Nose-to-tail horses

This photograph from the late 1800s shows why we talk about nose-to-tail traffic jams. Before cars were invented, most road transport was by horse-drawn carriage. City streets in those days could become just as jammed with vehicles as they do today.

WHEELS IN MOTION

B EFORE A CAR MOVES, the engine must change the up-and-down movement of the pistons into the round-and-round movement of a shaft (rod) that turns the wheels. With the engine running, the driver presses down the clutch and pushes the gear stick into first gear in the gearbox. The engine turns a shaft called a crankshaft. The power from the turning crankshaft is then transmitted through the gearbox to the wheels on the road. The combined movement makes the wheels on the road turn forwards. The wheels turn backwards when the driver pushes the gear stick into reverse gear.

This project shows you how to make a simple machine that creates a similar motion, where one kind of movement that goes round and round can be turned into another kind of movement that goes up and down.

Wind up
The earliest motor cars did not have a starter motor. The driver had to put a starting handle into the front of the car. This connected the handle to the engine's crankshaft to turn it. Turning the handle was hard work and could break the driver's arm if not done correctly. Button-operated starters began to be fitted as early as 1912.

CHANGING MOTION

You will need: *shoebox, thin metal rod about 2mm diameter, pliers, jam jar lid, adhesive tape, scissors, thick plastic straw, pencil, piece of stiff paper, at least four colour felt-tipped pens, thin plastic straw*

1 Place the shoebox narrow-side-down on a flat surface. With one hand push the metal rod through the centre, making sure your other hand will not get jabbed by the rod.

2 Bend the rod at right angles where it comes out of the box. Attach the jam jar lid to it with adhesive tape. Push the lid until it rests against the side of the box.

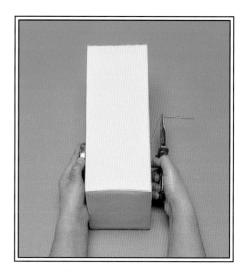

3 Carefully use the pliers to bend the piece of rod sticking out of the other side of the box. This will make a handle for the piston that will be able to turn easily.

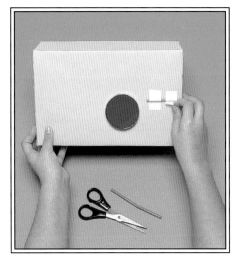

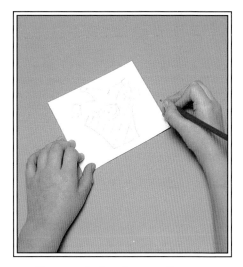

4 Cut a piece of thick plastic straw about 5cm long and tape it to the side of the box close to the jam jar lid. Make sure that it just sticks up beyond the edge of the box.

5 Draw a design in pencil on a piece of stiff paper. Copy the jester shown in this project or draw a simple clown. Choose something that looks good when it moves.

6 Using the felt-tipped pens, colour the design until it looks the way you want it to. The more colourful the figure is, the nicer it will look on the top of the piston.

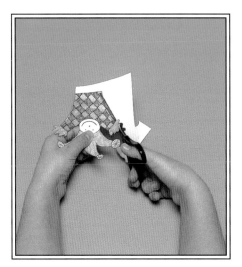

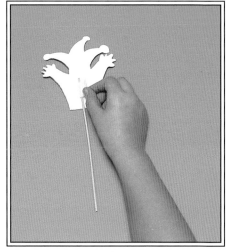

7 Carefully cut the finished drawing out of the paper. Make sure you have a clean-edged design. Try not to smudge the felt-tipped colour with your fingers.

8 Use the adhesive tape to attach the thin plastic straw to the bottom of the drawing. About 2cm of straw should be attached.

10 Place the box on end so the jester is at the top. Turn the handle on the left-hand side. As you turn, the jam jar lid revolves and pushes the jester up and down, like a piston.

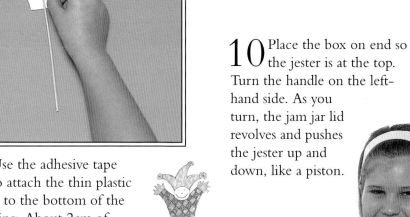

9 Slide the straw attached to the drawing into the straw taped to the back of the box. It will come out of the other end. Push down so that the straw touches the edge of the jam jar lid.

MASS PRODUCTION

ONCE WAYS had been found to power a small, wheeled road vehicle, more and more people wanted to own a car. Having one made getting around so much easier. However, early cars were built by hand, piece by piece, which took time. In 1903, the US inventor Henry Ford produced the Model A Ford, the first car designed to be built in large numbers. It gave him the idea to mass-produce all the separate parts of a car in the same place, then have his workers assemble many cars at the same time. This became known as the production-line method. By 1924, 10 million Ford cars had been built and sold. Today, almost all cars are built on production lines. Robots (automated machines) do much of the work. Some cars are still built by hand, but they can only be built very slowly. For example, the British sports-car maker Morgan made 11 cars a week in 1999. In comparison, the Ford Motor Company built about 138,000 cars a week in the same year.

Tin Lizzie
The Model T Ford was the world's first mass-produced (assembled on a production line) car. Millions were made and sold all over the world. Nowadays people collect examples of these cars, maintaining, restoring and repairing them, often to a gleaming state. It is unlikely that they would have been so well cared for by their original owners.

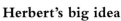

Herbert's big idea
The Austin Seven was one of the most popular cars ever. This version is a sporting two seater. Between 1922 and 1938 there were many versions, including racing cars and even vans. The Austin Motor Company was founded by Herbert Austin in 1903. The company allowed other car makers to build the Austin Seven in France, Japan, America and Germany.

Beetling about
In 1937, the German government founded a car company to build cheap cars. The car, designed by Dr Ferdinand Porsche, was called the Volkswagen, meaning 'people's car', but it gained the nickname of the 'Beetle' because of its unusual shape. Some people painted their Beetles for fun. By the 1960s, the car was popular worldwide. By 2000, over 21 million Volkswagens had been sold.

Next one, please

Modern cars are made with the help of machines in factories. Each machine does a different job. Some weld metal parts together, others attach fittings and secure fastenings, others spray paint. The car's metal body parts come together on a moving track that runs past each machine. Making cars like this means they can be put together quickly and in vast numbers.

FACT BOX

• Speedometers (dials showing a car's speed) were first used in cars in 1901.

• The American car maker Buick started life as a bath tub manufacturer.

• By 1936, more than 50 per cent of all US families owned a car.

Big yellow taxi

For people without a car, such as tourists, taxis are a convenient way of getting around in towns and cities. Taxi drivers try to find the best short cuts for an easy journey. Hiring a taxicab also means that people don't have to find a place to park. The bright yellow 'checker cabs' in New York, USA, became a symbol for the city all over the world, because everyone recognized them.

The people's servant

The Trabant was from East Germany. Many millions were built for ordinary people. Its name comes from a Hungarian word meaning 'servant', and the Trabant served as a cheap, reliable car across Eastern Europe. This 601 model was first made in 1964.

Alec's big idea

Launched in 1959, the Morris Mini Minor was one of the most revolutionary cars of the last 50 years. It was cheap to buy and cheap to run, easy to drive and easy to park. Despite its small size, it could carry four people comfortably. The car's designer, Alec Issigonis, a British citizen of Greek parentage, also designed the Morris Minor, a small family car launched in 1948.

THE ENGINE

A CAR'S ENGINE is made up of metal parts. They are designed to work together smoothly and efficiently. In older cars, a valve called a carburettor feeds a mixture of air and fuel into the cylinder, where the mixture is burnt to produce power. Newer cars often use an injection system, which measures and controls the amount of fuel into the engine more accurately. To keep the engine cool, water is pumped from the radiator and circulated around chambers in the cylinder block. The waste gases created by the burnt fuel are carried away by the exhaust system. The engine sucks in the air and petrol mixture and allows it to burn. To help the moving parts move against each other smoothly, they are lubricated with oil from the engine oil sump. A pump squirts the oil on to the parts.

A car's electrical power is driven by an alternator. The electrical current is stored in the battery. This provides the electricity for the spark that ignites the fuel mixture, for the car's electrical system, and for its heater, lights, radio, windscreen wipers and instruments.

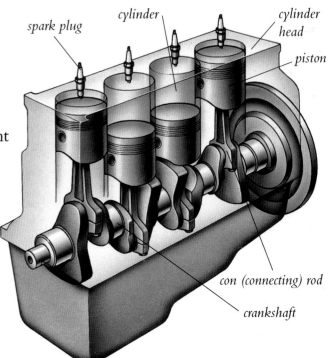

spark plug · cylinder · cylinder head · piston · con (connecting) rod · crankshaft

Working together

Most car engines have four cylinders. In each cylinder a piston moves up and down. Four rods, one from each piston, turn metal joints attached to the crankshaft. As the rods turn the joints, the crankshaft moves round and round. The movement is transmitted to the wheels, using the gearbox to control how fast the wheels turn relative to the engine.

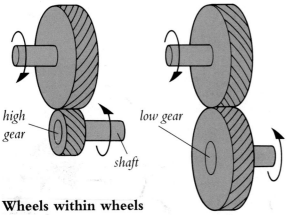

high gear · low gear · shaft

Wheels within wheels

The car's engine turns a shaft (rod) with different sized gears (toothed wheels) on it. High gears are used for more speed because when a big wheel turns a small one, it turns faster. The gear system is called the transmission, because it transmits (moves) the engine's power to the car's wheels. Many cars have five forward gears. The biggest is needed for slow speeds, and the smallest for high speeds. When the car goes round corners, its wheels move at different speeds. A set of gears called the differential allows the wheels to do this.

Turbo tornado

This 1997 Dodge engine can make a car go especially fast because it has a turbocharger that forces the fuel and air mixture faster and more efficiently into the engine cylinder head. Turbochargers are driven by waste exhaust gases drawn away from the exhaust system, which is a way of turning the waste gases to good use. Turbochargers are very effective at boosting engine power.

DODGE CUMMINS 5.9L I-6 INTERCOOLED TURBO-DIESEL
359 CU. IN. · 215 HP @ 2600 RPM (MANUAL) · 180 HP @ 2500 RPM (AUTO)
440 LB-FT TORQUE @ 1600 RPM (MANUAL)

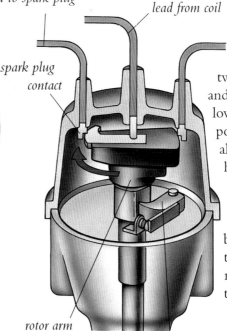

Power control
The distributor has two jobs. It connects and disconnects low-value electric power to the coil. It also supplies high-value electric power from the coil to each spark plug. This makes a spark big enough to ignite the air and fuel mixture at exactly the right time.

lead to spark plug

lead from coil

spark plug contact

rotor arm

contact breaker

What you see is what you get
This vintage racing Bentley displays its twin carburettors mounted on a supercharger (a mechanically driven device similar to a turbocharger) in front of the engine. The water pipes from the radiator to the engine, electric leads, plug leads and large open exhaust pipes can all be seen.

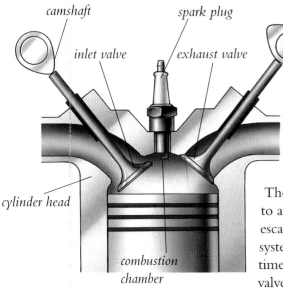

camshaft

spark plug

inlet valve

exhaust valve

cylinder head

combustion chamber

Double movement
The camshaft opens and closes the inlet and exhaust valves. The valves are fitted into the cylinder head, and open and close holes in the combustion chamber. The exhaust valve opens to allow burnt waste gases to escape into the car's exhaust system. The spark plug is timed to spark when both valves have closed both holes.

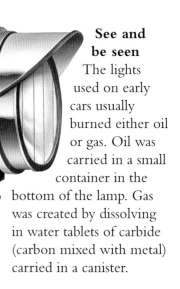

See and be seen
The lights used on early cars usually burned either oil or gas. Oil was carried in a small container in the bottom of the lamp. Gas was created by dissolving in water tablets of carbide (carbon mixed with metal) carried in a canister.

Blow them away
Mercedes-Benz fitted a supercharger to this 1936 540K to add power to the engine. The German company first used superchargers on their racing cars in 1927. This method of adding power had first been used on aeroplane engines in 1915.

IN THE RIGHT GEAR

GEARS ARE toothed wheels that interlock with each other to transfer movement. They have been used in machines of many kinds for over 2,000 years. In a car gearbox, the gears are arranged on shafts so that they interlock when the driver changes from one gear to the next. Cars have four, five or six forward gears according to the design, use and cost of the car. Several gears are needed because driving requires different combinations of speed and force at different times.

   The largest gear wheel is bottom gear. It turns slower than the higher gears. It provides more force and less speed for when the car is moving from stop, or going uphill. In top gear, less force and more speed is provided. This gear wheel is the smallest and rotates the fastest. The project connects two gears to show the beautiful patterns that gears can make. Then you can make your own three-gear machine.

Uphill struggle
Pushing a car up a steep hill in a 1920s car rally put a lot of strain on the low gears in a car. On steep slopes, first and second gears are often the only ones that a driver can use. Fourth gear is used for flat roads and fifth gear for cruising at high speeds.

DRAWING WITH GEARS

You will need: pair of compasses, A4 sheet of white paper, black pen, scissors, A4 sheet of thin cardboard, two strips of corrugated card, adhesive tape, three coloured felt-tipped pens.

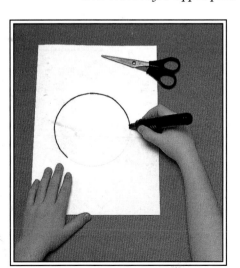

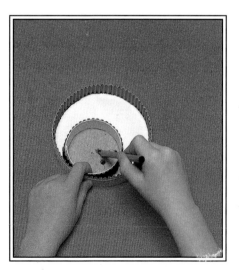

1 Using the pair of compasses, trace a 14cm diameter circle on the paper. Draw over it with the pen and cut it out. On the cardboard, trace, draw and cut out another circle with a diameter of 11cm.

2 Tape corrugated card around the circles, as shown. Make a hole in the small circle wide enough for the tip of a felt-tipped pen. Turn the small wheel inside the larger. Trace the path in felt-tipped pen.

3 Make a second hole in the small wheel. Turn the small gear inside the larger using another felt-tipped pen. Make a third hole in the small wheel and use a third colour pen to create an exciting, geometric design.

THREE-GEAR MACHINE

You will need: *pair of compasses, A4 sheet of cardboard, pen, scissors, three strips of corrugated card, adhesive tape, A4 piece of fibreboard, glue, 6cm piece of 12mm-diameter wood dowel, three map pins.*

1 Use the compasses to trace one 14cm diameter and two 11cm diameter circles in the cardboard. Draw around the circle edges with the pen and cut the circles out.

2 Carefully wrap the strips of corrugated card around the circles, using one strip per circle, corrugated side out. Tape each strip to the bottom of the circles.

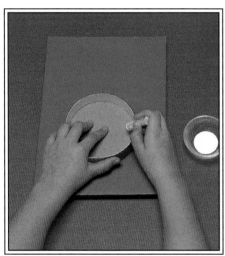

3 Place the largest gear wheel on the piece of fibreboard. Hold the gear down and glue the dowel on to the side of the gear base at the edge of the wheel. Leave it until it is dry.

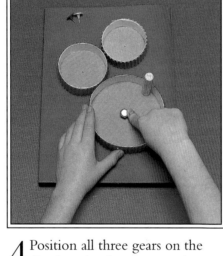

4 Position all three gears on the fibreboard, edges just touching each other. Pin each of them firmly to the fibreboard with a map pin but allow them to turn.

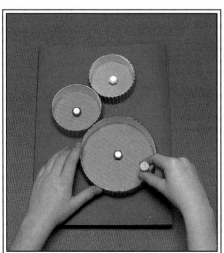

5 Gently turn the dowel on the largest gear. As that gear turns, the two others that are linked together by the corrugated card will turn against it. See how they move in opposite directions to each other.

6 Now you have a three-gear machine where the energy from each gear is being transferred to the other, just like the gears in a car.

SAFE RIDE AND HANDLING

MOST MODERN cars have four wheels. The wheels tend to be placed one at each corner, which helps to distribute the car's weight evenly on the road. An evenly balanced car rides and handles well and has good road grip and braking. Engine power usually drives either the front or rear wheels. However, with the growth in off-road driving in farming and for pleasure, all-wheel drive has become popular.

Driving safely at speed in a straight line or round corners is a test of how well a car has been designed. Many cars now have power-assisted steering to make steering easier. Tyres are an important part of good road handling. The tread pattern and grooves are designed to make the tyre grip the road efficiently, especially in wet, slippery conditions.

Big bopper
The French tyre manufacturer Michelin has been making tyres since 1888. The Michelin brand has been known for many years by the sign of a human figure that looks as though it is made out of tyres.

Gripping stuff
Tyre tread patters have raised pads, small grooves and water-draining channels to grip the road surface. There are different kinds of tyres for cars, buses, trucks and tractors. Tyre makers also make tyres for different road conditions. Examples include winter tyres and special run-flat tyres that stay hard even when they are damaged.

Dig deep
Tractor tyres are very deeply grooved. This allows them to grip hard in slippery mud. The width of the tyres spreads the weight of the heavy vehicle over soft ground. The tyres are high so that the tractor can ride easily over obstacles on the ground, such as big rocks.

Burn the rubber

Racing car tyres are wide so that the car can go as fast as possible while maintaining grip and stability on the road. They are made in various very hard mixtures of rubber to cope with different amounts of heat generated by racing in different conditions. Ordinary tyres would melt.

Out for a spin

Until very light alloy wheels became available in the last 20 years, sports cars often had wire-spoke wheels. These combined strength with lightness, both important features in a sports car. When a sports car brakes or turns sharply, modern wire-spoke wheels are strong enough to take the strain.

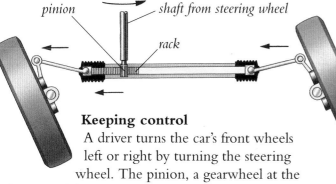

pinion   *shaft from steering wheel*

rack

Keeping control

A driver turns the car's front wheels left or right by turning the steering wheel. The pinion, a gearwheel at the bottom of the steering shaft, interlocks with a toothed rack. This is connected to the wheels via a system of joints and wheels. As the steering wheel turns, the movement of the pinion along the rack turns the road wheels.

King of the castle

Very large trucks that carry heavy loads use enormous tyres to spread the weight. This flatbed truck has been fitted with earthmover tyres for fun. Look how much bigger they are than the car the truck is rolling over.

Firm in the wet

Travelling at speed on a wet road can be dangerous. Water can form a film that is able to lift a tyre clear of the road surface for several seconds. To prevent this, tyre makers mould drain channels into the tyre's tread to push the water away from under the tyre as it rotates.

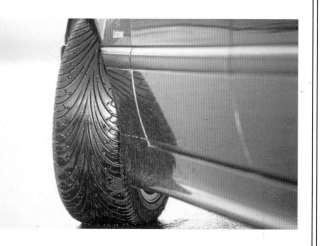

SPEED CONTESTS

RACING CARS against one another to test their speed and endurance has gone on for over 100 years. The American car maker Henry Ford, for example, designed and built racing cars before he set up the Ford car factory in 1903. Many kinds of car race now take place, including stock car, rally, speedway and drag racing. The FIA (*Fédération Internationale de l'Automobile*) makes rules about issues such as the tracks, the design and power of the cars, and the safety of drivers and spectators.

The fastest and most powerful kind of track racing is Formula One, also known as Grand Prix racing. The cars can travel up to 320km/hour on straight sections of track. Because the races are so exciting, the best drivers are paid in the millions. Formula One winners, such as David Coulthard and Michael Schumacher, are international celebrities. Technological advances in production-line cars have often been developed and tested in Grand Prix cars.

GRAND-PRIX Dieppe de l'A·C·F· 1907   NAZZARO sur F·I·A·T·

Your move
When racing drivers complete a race and cross the finishing line, a race official waves a black and white flag known as the chequered flag. The black and white pattern of squares on the finishing flag looks like the pattern on a chessboard. It is known all over the world as the sign of motor racing.

Monster motors
Early Grand Prix cars, such as this 10.2 litre Fiat, had enormous engines. Grand Prix racing began in France in 1904 and slowly spread to other countries. The *Association Internationale des Automobiles Clubs Reconnus* (AIACR) set the rules for races until it was reformed as the FIA in 1946.

Round the bend
The Italian car maker Ferrari has been making racing cars since 1940. Here the German Michael Schumacher, driving the Ferrari F399, rounds a curve on the 4.7km Catalunya circuit at the 1999 Barcelona Grand Prix.

FACT BOX

• Between 1980 and 1982, the French driver Alain Prost won 51 Formula One races, the highest number so far achieved by any Grand Prix driver.

• Ayrton Senna won the Monaco Grand Prix a record six times between 1987 and 1993.

• The racetrack at Indianapolis, USA, was known as "the brickyard" because it was partly paved with bricks until 1961.

Take-off

The speeds at which rally cars travel mean they often fly over the tops of the hills on the course. The driver and navigator of this car in the 1999 Portuguese Rally are strapped in to their seats to protect them from the tremendous thump that will come when the car's four wheels touch the ground in a second or two.

Take it to the limit

The heat generated by a Top Fuel drag racer's engine at the 1996 NHRA (*National Hot Rod Association*) Winternational makes the air vibrate around it. Drag races are short, like sprint races for athletes. The races take place over a straight course only 402m long, and the cars can reach speeds of 400km/hour. The flat spoilers on the front and rear of the cars are pushed down by the air rushing past, helping to keep the car on the road.

Making a splash

Rally car driving is extremely tough on the cars and on the drivers. Cars drive over deserts, mud-filled roads, rivers, snow and many other obstacles. The cars follow the same route, but start at different times. The course is divided into separate sections known as Special Stages. There is a time limit for each stage. The winner of the rally is the car that has the fastest overall time.

The chase

Tight bends are a test of driving skills for Formula One drivers. The cars brake hard from very high speeds as they approach the bend. Drivers try not to leave any gap that following cars could use for overtaking. As the drivers come out of the bend they accelerate as hard as is possible without skidding and going into a spin.

Thrill becomes spill

The Brazilian Mauricio Gugelmin's car soars into the air at the 1985 French Grand Prix, crashing to the ground upside down. The driver survived and has since taken part in many Grand Prix races. Safety regulations have improved in recent years.

RACE TRACKS

People have been racing cars on specially designed public circuits (tracks) almost since cars were invented. The first race on a special circuit took place in 1894 in France. The Italian track at Monza is one of the oldest racing circuits. It was built for the 1922 Italian Grand Prix. Among the most well-known tracks are Silverstone and Brands Hatch in Great Britain, Indianapolis in the USA, the Nürburgring in Germany, and Monaco. Millions of people all over the world watch the races at these tracks and on television. The teams and the drivers compete furiously with one another to prove whose car is the fastest. Sometimes the competition can be so fierce it is deadly. Ayrton Senna, a top Brazilian racing driver, died in a fatal crash at Imola in Italy in 1994. In this project, you can build your own race track, specially designed to let your cars build up speed on a steep slope, and race against a partner to see whose car is the fastest.

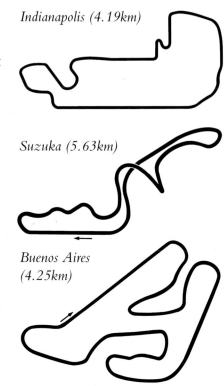

Indianapolis (4.19km)

Suzuka (5.63km)

Buenos Aires (4.25km)

TESTING GROUND

You will need: *25cm of 8cm-diameter cardboard tube, scissors, small paintbrush, blue paint, three strips of coloured paper 6cm x 2cm, adhesive tape, two strips of white paper 1.5cm x 8cm, pencil, red and black felt-tipped pen, pieces of coloured and white paper, cocktail sticks, A4 sheet of stiff red card, ruler, two small model cars.*

Twist and turn

All racetracks, such as those shown above, test the skill of the drivers and the speed and handling of the racing cars. They combine bends with straight stretches. Sharp bends are known as hairpin bends. Most tracks are between 4 and 5.5km in length.

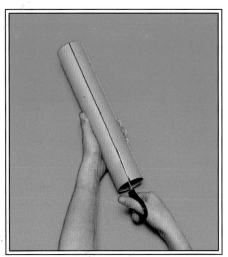

1 Use the scissors to carefully cut the cardboard tube in half along its length. Hold the tube in one hand but make sure you keep the scissor blades away from your hands.

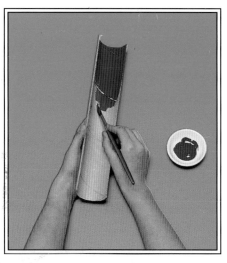

2 Use the paintbrush to apply a thick coat of blue paint to the inside of both halves of the tube. To give a strong colour, paint a second coat after the first has dried.

3 Use adhesive tape to stick the ten narrow strips of coloured paper together. Tape them along their widths to make a flexible bend. This joins the racetrack together.

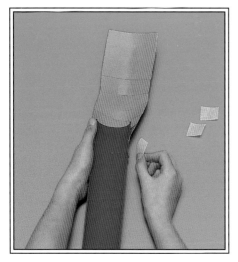

4 Now take the flexible bend you have made from strips of paper. Tape it to one end of one of the painted halves of the tube. Use small pieces of adhesive tape.

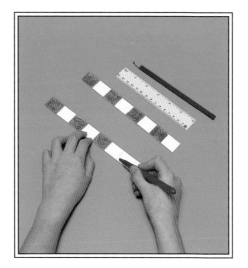

5 Use a pencil to mark eight equal 1cm blocks on both of the strips of white paper. Colour in alternate red blocks with a felt-tipped pen to make striped crash barriers.

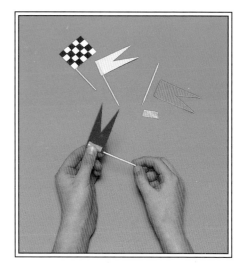

6 Colour in a 4cm x 8cm piece of paper with 1cm black and white squares. Cut the other paper pieces into pennants (forked flags). Tape the flags to cocktail sticks.

7 Cut three 8cm-wide strips from the sheet of stiff card. Use scissors to cut a semicircle out of the top of each of the strips.

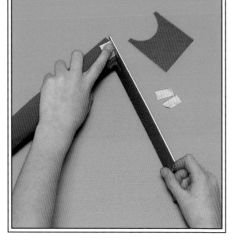

8 Measure with a ruler and cut the three strips to varying heights of 20cm, 14cm and 7cm. Tape them to the underside of half of the tube, fitting them on at the semicircle shapes to support the half tube in a gradual slope.

9 Tape the second half of the tube to the end of the flexible bend. Put in the crash barriers. Now you are ready to roll your toy car down the death-defying slope of your racetrack. Make another racetrack with a friend and you can race each other's cars.

Popping the cork
Race winners Canadian Jacques Villeneuve and Frenchman Jean Alesi celebrate by showering each other with champagne at the Luxembourg Grand Prix in 1997.

COLLECTING

The cars that were made many years ago have not been forgotten. They are known as veteran (made before 1905), Edwardian (1905–1919), vintage (1919–1930) and Classics. Enthusiasts (people with a special interest) all over the world collect and maintain old cars. They value them for many reasons, such as the great care that went into making them, their design, their engine power and their rarity. Clubs such as the AACA (Antique Automobile Club of America) and FIVA (*Fédération Internationale des Véhicules Anciens*) exist for the collectors of old American and European cars. There are also specific clubs for owners of particular models of car. Owners like to meet up and compare notes on maintaining their vehicles. Their clubs organize tours and rallies in which owners can drive their cars in working order.

Annual get together
Veteran cars (built before 1905) parade along the sea front in Brighton, England. The London-to-Brighton veteran car run has been held every year (except during wartime) since 1904. It celebrates cars being driven without someone with a red flag walking in front to warn of their approach.

Who stole the roof?
Early vehicles were built on the frames of horse-drawn wagons, so they had little protective bodywork. Drivers and their passengers had to wrap up well when driving.

Room for two?
Frenchman Louis Delage built cars of great engineering skill. The engine of this 1911 racing model was so big that there was little room for the driver. The huge tube in the bonnet carried exhaust gases to the back of the car.

High roller

The Rolls–Royce Silver Ghost is one of the great early vintage cars. It was first built in 1906. Almost 8,000 were made before production finally stopped in 1925. By that time, fewer people were able to afford such large, expensive cars. Individual buyers could have the car's specification and equipment altered according to their own needs. Several Silver Ghosts were produced as armoured cars to protect top British Army generals during World War I.

Mighty midget

The 1930 MG Midget was a powerful small car and clearly deserved its name. The Midget was the first car that the MG company sold in large numbers. Its success allowed the firm to expand and become more widely known.

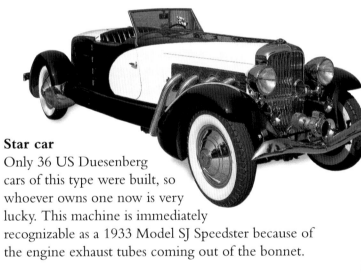

Star car

Only 36 US Duesenberg cars of this type were built, so whoever owns one now is very lucky. This machine is immediately recognizable as a 1933 Model SJ Speedster because of the engine exhaust tubes coming out of the bonnet.

Mint condition

The owners of old cars have to give a great deal of loving care to the car engines. Keeping an original MG Midget engine running demands patience in finding spare parts, maintaining old metal and making regular tests.

Starry Ferrari

The Italian company Ferrari is one of the world's greatest car makers. Owning a Ferrari has always been seen as a symbol of wealth and success, so the cars are favourites with film stars and sports stars. This 166 Ferrari is from the late 1940s.

In demand

A 1930s racing car combines style and power, qualities that still give Alfa Romeo its strong reputation. Collectors today value racing cars of the past just as much as old passenger cars. The Italian car maker Alfa Romeo has been building fast cars since 1915.

OFF-ROAD VEHICLES

M OST CARS are designed for driving on smooth roads. There are specialized vehicles, however, that can drive across rough terrain such as mud, desert and stony ground. Usually called off-road vehicles (ORVs) or All-Terrain Vehicles (ATVs), cars of this kind often have four-wheel drive, large tyres and tough suspension. They stand high off the ground and have strong bodywork. The earliest ORVs were the US Jeep and the British Land Rover. The Jeep, made by Ford and Willys, started life in World War II. It was designed to travel across roads damaged by warfare. The Land Rover, built by the Rover company in the late 1940s, was based on the idea of the Jeep. It was intended for farmers, who have to drive across difficult terrain. The Land Rover proved useful in all parts of the world where roads were poor or non-existent. Travelling off-road is still a necessity in many places. However, in recent times, it has beome a popular leisure activity for some drivers, who like to test their driving skills on difficult terrain.

Seaside fun
Driving on beaches is difficult because wheels can sink into the wet sand. Vehicles for driving on beaches are built to be very light, with balloon tyres to spread the vehicle's weight over a wide area.

Tough cookie
At the start of World War II the US Army developed a vehicle with a sturdy engine, body and framework. The wheels were at the corners for stability over rough ground. The GP (General Purpose) vehicle became known as the Jeep.

No traffic jams
The Lunar Rover, carried to the Moon by *Apollo 17* in 1971, was powered by electricity. The low gravity of the moon meant that it would not sink into soft ground. A wide track and long wheelbase stopped it from turning over if it hit a rock.

Angel of mercy

Vehicles such as Jeeps help doctors to take medical aid to people living in remote areas where there are few roads. A four-wheel drive vehicle, it can cross shallow rivers and rough terrain. A specially toughened underbody protects against damage from water.

Hospital on wheels

Aid agencies such as UNICEF and *Mèdecins Sans Frontières* use specially adapted trucks fitted out as mobile hospitals. They help to save lives in times of war and natural disaster. Heavily reinforced bodywork protects patients and easily damaged medical supplies.

Electric caddies

A typical game of golf involves travelling five kilometres or more. Golfers need an easy way to carry heavy golf clubs around the course. Golf karts (also called golf buggies) are simple, light vehicles powered by electricity. They have enough battery life to carry golfers and their clubs from the first to the last hole on the course.

FACT BOX

• The 11,000km Paris-Dakar-Cairo Rally is one of the world's best-known off-road races. Founded in 1978 by the French driver Thierry Sabine, the year 2000 race had 600 team members driving 200 motorbikes, 141 cars and 65 trucks.

Get tracking

Half-tracks played an important part in World War II, and still do in modern warfare. They have tracks at the rear to allow them to travel over very broken surfaces such as roads filled with shell holes and debris. The wheels at the front give half-tracks an added mobility that tanks do not have.

Big boss

Large, high, off-the-road cars such as the Mitsubishi Shogun and commercial ORVs grew increasingly popular from the 1980s. They had four-wheel drive, which made driving on rough ground much easier.

CUSTOM-BUILT

SOMETIMES SERIOUS car enthusiasts decide to adapt a standard model. They might alter the engine to make it run faster, or change the body to make it look different. Cars specially adapted like this are known as custom cars. Custom cars have become very popular since the 1950s, particularly in the USA. The wheels may be taken from one kind of car, the body from a second, the mudguards and engine from others, and the different parts are combined to make a completely original car. The end result can be dramatic. These unusual cars have many different names, such as mean machines, street machines, muscle machines and hot rods. Racing custom cars is a popular activity. Stock cars are custom cars built especially for races in which crashes often occur. Drag racers are incredibly fast and powerful cars built for high speed races over short distances.

Water baby
Surf's up and the muscle machine is on the tideline. This cool dude has fitted big, wide tyres on a roadster body to spread the car's weight on soft sand. He has been busy with a paintbrush, too, adding flames to his body paint.

Made to measure
This car is a mixture of styles. The driver's cab and steering wheel have been made to look like those in a veteran car. The modern engine is chrome-plated, with all the parts visible. The exhaust-outlet tubes resemble those from a 1930s racing car. The front wheels are bigger than the rear ones.

Soft furnishings
Some people change the insides of their cars to create a truly luxurious look. They replace the standard fittings, for example, with soft leather seats, padded dashboards and chrome-covered gear shifts.

Smokin' steady
The grille on the bonnet of a customized hot rod is the turbocharger. It can boost the engine to speeds of 400km/hour. When the car brakes at high speed, its tyres make lots of smoke because they are burning from friction with the road.

FLUFFY DICE

You will need: *cuboid box at least 12cm square, two A4 sheets of white paper, adhesive tape, scissors, 20cm length of string, 80cm square of furry fabric, pencil, bradawl, glue, circle stencil.*

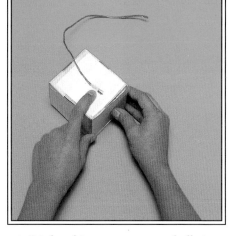

1 Stick white paper around all six surfaces of the box with tape. Use a small piece of adhesive tape to stick 3cm of the end of the length of string to one side of the box.

2 Place the fabric furry-side down. Place the box at one edge and draw around it. Then roll the box over and draw around it again. Do six squares like this to form a cross.

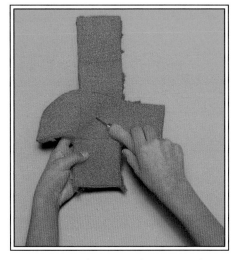

3 Cut out the cross shape. With a bradawl, carefully make a hole in the fur. Place the box face down on the fur where the string is attached. Pull the string through the hole.

4 Spread glue evenly on the inside of each square of the fabric, one at a time. Press the glued material squares on to the box faces.

5 Choose a medium-sized circle shape from the circle stencil. Using a pencil, draw 21 of the same circles on to the piece of white paper.

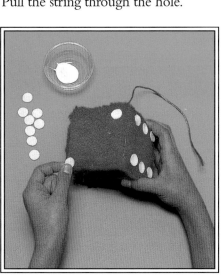

6 Cut out the circles. Glue them on to the furry side of the fabric. Put six dots on one face, five dots on the next, then four, three, two and finally one dot. You could use a real dice to see the correct arrangement.

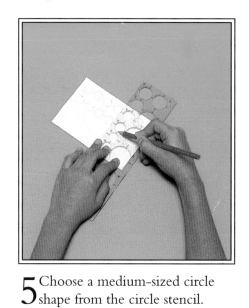

7 Make a second die and hang them in the car for fun. Put them where they will not distract the driver. They should not hang on the windows.

UNUSUAL DESIGNS

CARS ARE often adapted (have their design changed) to suit different needs, or just for fun. Three-wheeled cars, a kind of microcar, are cheap to run and take up less road space than the conventional four-wheeled cars.

Amphibious vehicles that can operate on land and water were built in World War II for fighting. Since then, specialist German, British and Chinese manufacturers have gone on building small numbers of these cars for use in regions with many rivers.

Film studios often create sensational special effects around cars that appear to have special powers. Then there are the real but completely wacky cars, made by people who want to create cars that defy the imagination. These have included cars that split down the middle, cars that are covered in fur, and cars that look like sofas and cans of baked beans.

Frog face
The microcars produced in in the 1950s and 1960s were for driving in towns. This 1959 Messerschmitt had a tiny engine and was just 2.7m long. Even so, it had a top speed of 100km/hour. The top of the car swings over to allow the driver entry. The car was also very cheap to run. It used only one litre of petrol every 24km, almost half the fuel consumption of an average modern car.

Garden car
This car may look like a garden shed, but in order to travel on a public road it needs to conform to all the regulations of the road. It will have passed an annual inspection for safety and roadworthiness. Headlights, indicators and safety belts are all fitted.

Supermarket beep
A giant supermarket trolley has been constructed and fitted with a car engine. This vehicle is strictly for fun. Lacking basic safety features such as proper seats, lights and bumpers, it is not allowed to be driven on public roads.

Only in the movies

The 1977 James Bond film, *The Spy Who Loved Me*, featured a car that behaved as though it was also a submarine. It was a British Lotus Elite car body specially altered to create the illusion.

Magic car

Ian Fleming, the creator of James Bond, also wrote a book about a magic car. This became the 1968 film *Chitty Chitty Bang Bang*. The car was an old one that the book's hero, Caractacus Potts, discovered in a junkyard. After restoring it, he discovered it could fly and float.

FACT BOX

• One of the amphibious vehicles used in World War II was called a 'duck' after the initials DUKW given it by the manufacturer, US General Motors. It had six wheels and moved through the water powered by a propeller.

• Microcars, such as the BMW Isetta and the Heinkel Trojan, were also known in the 1950s and 1960s as bubble cars because of their round shapes and large window spaces.

• Race tracks such as Le Mans in France, and Monza in Italy, hosted race meetings in the 1950s and 1960s at which microcars such as the British Berkeley and the Italian Fiat Bianchina raced against each other.

Replica style

This 3-wheeler Triking, a modern replica (copy) of a 1930s Morgan, is a kit car that has been put together. The owner is supplied with all the different body panels and engine parts, and builds the complete car. Kit cars are cheaper than production-line cars, because the costs of assembly and labour are saved.

Web-toed drivers

Cars that can cross water are useful, especially in places where there are rivers but no bridges. Between 1961 and 1968, the German Amphicar company made almost 4,000 amphibious cars. They could reach a speed of 11km/hour in the water, pushed along by a Triumph Herald engine and two small propellers. On land they could reach 112km/hour.

COOLING SYSTEM

THE EXPLOSIONS in a car's engine, and the friction caused by its moving parts, create a great deal of heat. If the heat were not kept down, the engine would stop working. The metal parts would expand, seize up and stop. To cool the engine, water from a radiator is pumped through chambers in the cylinder block. The moving water carries heat away from the hottest parts of the engine. The radiator has to be cooled down too. A fan blows air on to it, to cool the water inside. The fan is driven by a belt from the engine crankshaft pulley. This project shows you how to transfer the energy of turning motion from one place to another. It uses a belt to move five reels. In the same way, some of the turning motion of an engine is transferred by a fan belt to the fan.

Rear engine
The air-cooled rear-engined Volkswagen Beetle was designed with an aerodynamic front and no need for a front-mounted radiator. Instead, the engine is cooled by a fan driven by a fan belt, like the one shown here. Engines of this kind are useful in cold climates, where low temperatures can freeze water in radiators.

FAN BELT

You will need: *ruler, 16cm square of thin cloth, scissors, five cotton reels, A4 wooden board, glue or glue stick, pencil, five flat-headed nails 4cm in length, hammer, 1m length of 2.5cm-wide velvet ribbon, sticky tape, pair of compasses, five pieces of 15cm-square coloured card, five wooden skewers.*

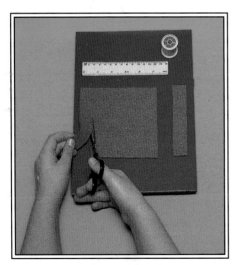

1 Using the ruler, measure five 2.5cm-wide strips on the thin cloth. The height of the cotton reels should be more than 2.5cm. Use the scissors to cut out each strip.

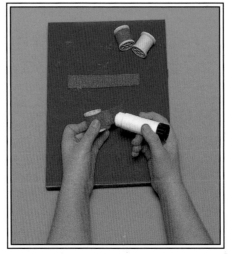

2 Wrap one of the fabric strips around each of the five cotton reels. Glue each strip at the end so that it sits firmly around the reel and does not come loose.

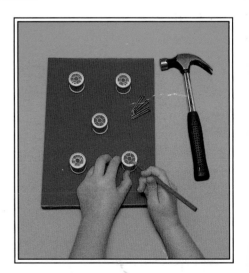

3 Place the reels on the wooden board as shown above. Trace the outlines with a pencil. Put the nails through the centre of the reels and carefully hammer them into the board.

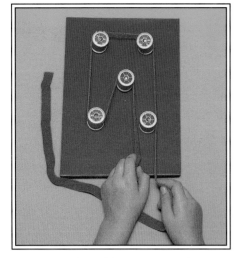

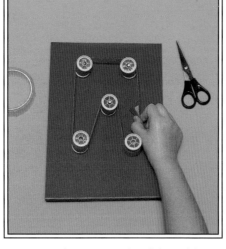

4 Wind the ribbon around the reels with the velvet side against four of the reels. Cut the ribbon at the point where you can join both ends round the fifth reel.

5 Tape the two ends of the ribbon together firmly. Make sure that the ribbon wraps firmly around all of the five reels, but not so tightly that it can not move.

6 Use the pair of compasses to draw circles about 7cm in diameter on to the pieces of coloured card. Then draw freehand spiral shapes inside each circle.

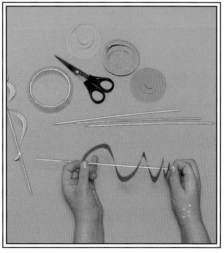

10 Now you are ready to turn the belt. Like a fan belt in a car, it turns the fans around. This is a five-fan machine. You can add more fans if you like.

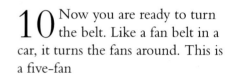

7 Use the scissors to cut each spiral out of each of the pieces of coloured card. Start from the outside edge and gradually work your way in along the lines of the spiral.

8 Tape one end of the spiral to the end of a skewer. Wind the other end of the spiral around the skewer stick a few times. Tape it close to the opposite end of the skewer.

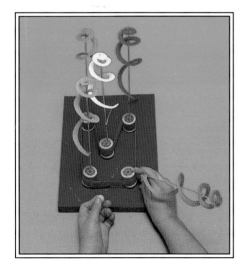

9 Put a small amount of sticky tape on the end of each skewer. Then place each skewer into one of the empty holes in the top of each cotton reel.

ENVIRONMENT MATTERS

CARS ARE convenient, but their effect on the environment causes concern. The manufacture, and the driving of cars both use up precious natural resources such as metals and oil. The emissions (waste gases) that petrol cars produce pollute the atmosphere. One of them, carbon monoxide, is thought by many scientists to be contributing to problems such as global warming (the warming of the world's climate because of gases trapped in the atmosphere).

Although the environmental problems associated with cars are many, car makers have made many improvements to their models during recent years. Cars are much lighter than they used to be, so smaller amounts of raw materials are needed to make them. Because they are lighter and their engines are more efficient, they can drive many more kilometres per litre of fuel than previously. In many countries, the emission of carbon monoxide into the atmosphere is actually lower now than twenty years ago, despite there being many more cars.

Costly accident
The petrol that cars burn is extracted from oil pumped out of the ground or from under the sea. The oil is transported in enormous ships to refineries where the petrol is extracted. Occasionally, a tanker sinks or is holed. When this happens, oil seeps into the sea and forms a slick on the surface, killing and injuring fish and birds.

FACT BOX

• Ford launched the Ford Fiesta in 1976, and the Ford Ka in 1998. Both are small runaround cars. But the exhaust gases of the 1976 Ford Fiesta contained fifty times more pollutants such as carbon monoxide and nitrogen oxides than the 1998 Ford Ka.

Route guidance
Traffic police may gradually be replaced by computerized route guidance technology called Telematics. In-car navigation systems and traffic messaging (radio messages on traffic conditions) enable drivers to use the best route. This can reduce journey times, and petrol consumption, by 10 per cent.

Going nowhere fast

There are too many cars in the world. Traffic congestion is a common experience for many. Transport experts are trying to link public transport with car use to reduce the problem. For example, park-and-ride schemes allow drivers to park near a town centre, then catch a free bus into the centre.

Rubber bounces back

The treads (gripping patterns) on tyres wear away until the tyre is too smooth to grip the road. Car owners throw away the old tyres and buy new ones. Like metal and plastic, rubber does not bio-degrade (decay naturally) easily. Tyres can be reused by being shredded and turned into tiny chips of rubber. These can be melted down to make asphalt for covering roads.

Plug-in car

Electric cars create much less pollution than petrol cars. They run off electricity stored in batteries. The batteries need to be recharged regularly by being plugged into the mains electricity supply. In parts of the USA such as California, drivers can find recharging stations in public places. Seven hours of charging will allow a car to travel a distance of about 160km.

On the scrapheap

Most of the materials used in cars can be recycled. Car companies are using more and more recycled materials in their new cars, such as old batteries to make new batteries, and plastic fittings to make new plastic-based parts. However, it is still very expensive to recycle the metal, so many old cars end up on scrapheaps.

Lights in the smog

Fumes from petrol cars cause smog over the city of Los Angeles. This is dangerous to people's health. Scientists are constantly researching alternative fuels. CNG (compressed natural gas) cars, which are already on sale, produce 20 percent less emissions than petrol cars.

BRAKING SYSTEMS

CARS HAVE two types of brakes. Parking brakes lock the rear wheels when the car is standing still. They are controlled by the handbrake lever inside the car. Brakes for when the car is moving are usually made of steel discs fixed to each wheel. They are called disc brakes and are controlled by the brake pedal inside the car. The disc brakes attached to the car's road wheels work just like the model disc brake in the project. Putting the brakes on too sharply when a car is moving can cause a skid, when the wheels lock and the tyres slide on the road surface.

Antilock braking systems (ABS), now used in many cars, measure the road surface conditions and stop the car going into a skid. This is done by making the disc brakes come on and off very quickly, so that the wheels cannot lock.

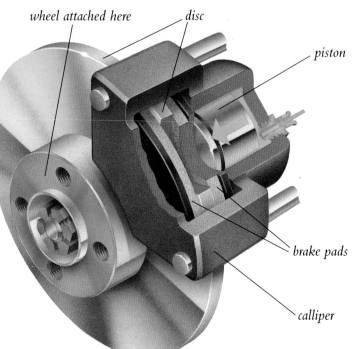

wheel attached here   *disc*   *piston*   *brake pads*   *calliper*

Squeeze, please
The disc brake unit's disc is attached to a turning hub This is bolted to the road wheel. When the driver presses the brake pedal, fluid is squeezed down a tube to the piston on the side of the disc brake. The piston presses together two pads, one on either side of the disc, gripping it firmly and stopping it from turning. As the disc slows, so does the car wheel.

Ready, steady, go
A stock car (modified saloon car) moves off from stop very suddenly. The driver builds up the power in the engine. When the engine is near full power, the driver quickly releases the brakes. Because the wheels suddenly start spinning incredibly quickly, the tyres roar and whine against the hard ground, and burn with the heat of the friction (rubbing) against the road. The burning rubber turns into smoke which billows in white clouds around the rear wheels.

Water sports
Rally drivers have to deal with extreme conditions such as dirt tracks, mud, snow and water. Powerful brakes help them to keep control of the cars. After going through water, a rally car's brakes would be wet. This makes them less effective because there is less friction. The brake pads slip against the wet disc. The driver has to press the brake pedal with a pumping action to get rid of the water.

DISC BRAKE

You will need: *scissors, 40cm length of fabric, circular cardboard box with lid, adhesive tape, pencil, 20cm length of 12mm-diameter wood dowel, glue, 7cm x 11cm piece of medium sandpaper, 6cm x 10cm wood block, two plastic cups, insulation tape.*

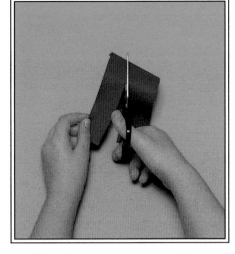

1 Use the scissors to cut a 40cm long strip from the fabric. You may have to use special fabric cutting scissors if ordinary scissors are not sharp enough.

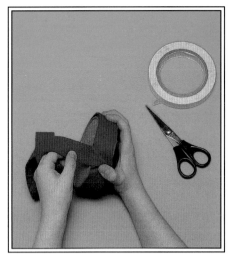

2 Take the strip of fabric you have cut out and wrap it around the rim of the circular cardboard box. Secure it firmly in place with small pieces of adhesive tape.

3 Make a hole in the centre of the box's lid with a pencil. Twist the pencil until it comes through the base of the box. Now gently push the wood dowel through both holes.

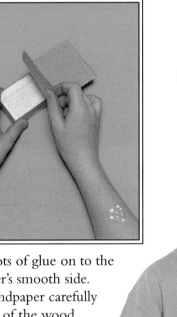

4 Spread lots of glue on to the sandpaper's smooth side. Wrap the sandpaper carefully over the top of the wood block, pressing to stick it.

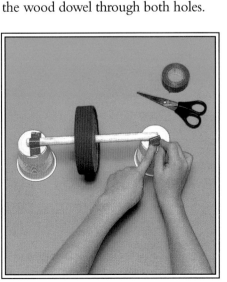

5 Stand two plastic cups upside down on a flat surface. Rest either end of the wooden dowel on each cup. Cut two small pieces of insulation tape. Use them to fix each end of the dowel firmly to the cup tops.

6 Spin the lid fast on the dowel. As it spins, bring the sandpaper into contact with the edge of the lid and see how it stops the lid turning. Test your brake disc and see how quickly and how gradually you can stop the lid.

SAFETY ISSUES

TRAFFIC ACCIDENTS are a constant danger. As the number of cars on the roads increased in the first half of the 1900s, the number of accidents to pedestrians and drivers increased also. During the last 50 years, ideas were put forward to reduce the scale of the problem. Gradually, most countries have decided that a driver must pass a test in driving skills. Governments have created safety regulations for road builders and car makers to follow. In many places, drivers and passengers are required by law to wear seat belts, and driving while under the influence of alcohol is forbidden in most countries.

New cars often have built-in safety features such as car body parts that resist crushing, and airbags that inflate to lessen the impact of collisions. Emergency road services deal more quickly with injured people. All these advances mean that in many countries there are now fewer road deaths than there were 20 years ago, even though there are more cars.

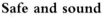

Safe and sound
If a car travelling at the relatively slow speed of 30km/hour stopped suddenly, a child could be thrown forwards and injured. To prevent this, a child can be strapped into a specially designed chair that is fixed securely to a car seat. It also stops the child from distracting the driver.

Bags of life
Experts who test cars for safety use crash-test dummies that react just like human bodies. These dummies are being protected by airbags, which were introduced into European production-line cars by Volvo in the 1980s. Airbags act as a kind of life-saving cushion, protecting a person from being thrown into the dashboard or the seat in front. The airbags inflate with gases as soon as sensors detect the first moment of a collision.

Not a care in the world
In the early days of motoring, people were much less aware of road safety as there were very few cars. In this 1906 drawing, a rich young man-about-town leans over the back of his car seat. He does not have to worry about where he is going because he has a chauffeur to drive him. Yet even the chauffeur is careless and narrowly avoids hitting a pedestrian in front of the car.

Pain in the neck

When a car stops suddenly, a person's head is jolted forwards and then sharply backwards. This can cause damage to the neck called whiplash. It often results in serious injury. Car manufacturers have invented seats that slide backwards and then tilt. The pictures show (1) the seat in normal position, (2) the seat sliding back, and (3) the seat's backrest tilting over. Combined with the headrest at the top, this seat design helps reduce whiplash.

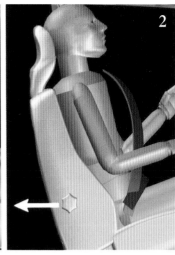
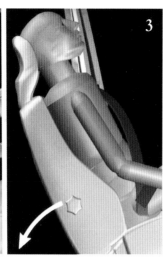

Traffic control

Before traffic control measures were introduced, accidents were common. In 1914, the first electric traffic light was installed in Cleveland, Ohio, USA. Traffic lights control the flow of cars through road junctions.

Grand slam

When cars collide with each other at high speed their bodywork (outer metal shell) smashes and twists. Safety engineers test the strength of a car's bodywork by hitting sample cars with powerful robot sledges. Wires attached to the car detect information about safety weak points. This information is used to improve the safety of materials and designs used in cars.

Major obstruction ahead

When a large truck tips over and spills its cargo, it creates all kinds of problems. Fire crews rescue anyone who is trapped in a vehicle, and medical teams treat any injured people. The police and fire crews direct the removal of the spilt cargo. Heavy cranes are needed to shift the truck. Although drivers are diverted to other routes, traffic jams build up that can stretch for long distances.

GOOD DESIGN

CAR MAKERS use large teams of people to create their new cars. Stylists, design engineers and production engineers combine with the sales team to develop a car that people will want to buy. Before the new car is announced to the public, models are made. A quarter-sized clay model is tested in a wind tunnel to investigate the car's aerodynamics (how air flows over its shape). Finally, a prototype (early version) of the car is built and tested for road handling, engine quality and comfort.

Painting on wheels
An old Mini Minor has been painted in exciting bright designs. A car's paintwork is called its livery.

Sleek and shiny
CAD (computer-aided design) software allows car designers to create a three-dimensional image of a new car design that can be looked at from any angle.

MODEL CAR

You will need: *two A4 sheets of cardboard, pair of compasses, ruler, scissors, glue, brush, bradawl, 15cm square piece of coloured card, pliers, 4 paper clips, two 10cm lengths of 12mm diameter wood dowel, sticky tape.*

Wire basket
Three-dimensional, wire-frame (see-through) computer images allow designers to see how the shapes of the car fit together.

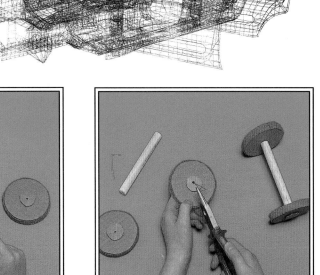

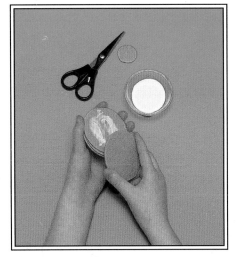

1 Draw and cut out four 2.5cm and eight 6cm diameter card circles. Glue the 6cm circles together to make four wheels. Glue a 2.5cm circle to the centre of each wheel.

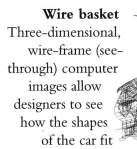

2 Use the bradawl to make a hole in the centre of each wheel. Cut four 4mm strips of coloured card. Wrap one each around the wheel rims. Glue the overlapping ends.

3 Push straightened paper clips into the holes and bend the outer ends with pliers. Fix the wheels to the two pieces of dowel by pushing the paper clips into the ends.

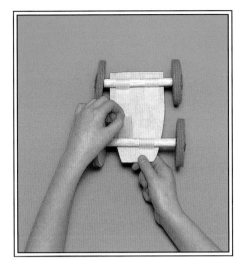

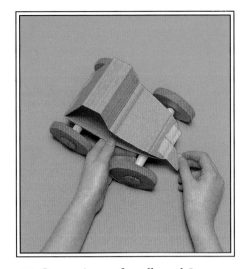

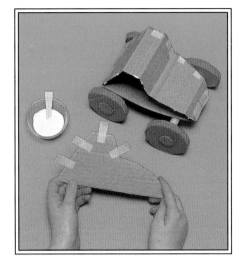

4 Cut a piece of cardboard 8cm x 15cm. Trim one end to make it 6cm wide. Tape the two axles to the board, one at each end. Leave space for the wheels to rotate freely.

5 Cut a piece of cardboard 8cm x 35cm. Double it over and bend it into a cab shape. Tape the two loose ends together. Stick the base of the cab shape to the car base.

6 Cut two cardboard shapes 15cm long x 10cm high. Trim them with the scissors to the same shape as the side of your car cab. Attach the sides to the cab with sticky tape.

DECORATE YOUR CAR

You will need: two colours of acrylic paints, medium paintbrushes, pencil, three pieces of A5 coloured card, a piece of white card, two colours of felt-tipped pens, scissors, glue.

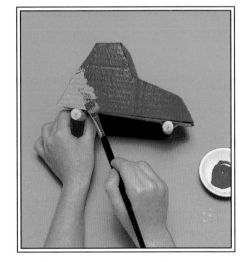

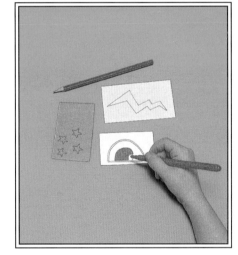

1 Remove the wheels from your car. Paint the sides and top of the cab with one of the two colours of paint. Paint two coats and leave to dry.

2 Draw exciting designs for the sides of the car, and a driver to go behind the windscreen. Colour them in with the felt-tipped pens.

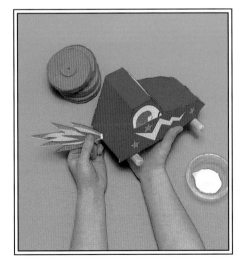

3 Let the paint dry for a couple of hours. Cut the designs out of the card. Glue them to the sides and back of the car. Paint the wheels with the colour of paint not yet used.

4 Replace the wheels when they are dry. Now your car looks just like a real street machine. Cut photographs of cars from magazines for ideas for new designs.

FRICTION AND OIL

WHEN THE parts of an engine move, they touch and create friction (rub against one another). The more quickly and often they move, the more friction there is. This makes the engine parts grow hot, but if they become too hot they expand and no longer fit properly. When this happens, the parts jam against one another and the engine seizes up.

Oil, a slippery liquid, lubricates the car engine. It is stored in a part of the engine, from where it is pumped onto the moving parts. Eventually the oil gets dirty with soot and bits of dirt from outside. The dirty oil must be drained, and clean oil put in at regular intervals. Ball bearings help other moving parts of the car turn against each other. The project shows you how marbles can behave like ball bearings to reduce friction.

Oil giant

Car ownership grew steadily in the 1930s. This created a big demand for new car products. People wanted to keep their cars running smoothly and safely. Most of all, car owners needed engine oil that was always high quality, wherever and whenever they bought it. Oil companies spent a lot of money on advertisements, telling people that their oil was the best.

Sea changes

Oil rigs drill deep into the sea-bed to find crude (natural) oil. Car lubricating oil is made from this. Pumps in the rig draw the crude oil up from the sea-bed into pipes leading to refineries on land. Impurities are removed from the crude oil in the refineries. This makes it light enough to use in car engines.

Extra Jag

High-performance sports cars such as the Jaguar E-Type of the 1960s need a particularly light oil. Otherwise their powerful engines will not run smoothly. The E-Type engine in this car has six cylinders (most car engines have four). They generate the power needed to accelerate to a top speed of 240km/hour. Over time a thick oil would clog the oil ways, leading to friction and wear and tear of many engine parts.

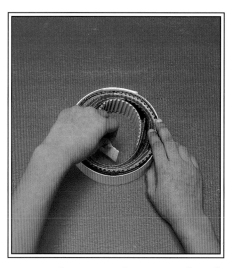

Oil guzzler
Large luxury cars
need a lot of oil.
This 1958 Lincoln
Continental has a huge
8-cylinder engine to lubricate.
During the 1950s oil was very
cheap. American car makers had less reason to think about the costs
of running cars as carefully as they have in more recent years.

Beetle's brother
Between 1955 and 1974,
Karmann produced the Karmann
Ghia cabriolet for the car maker
Volkswagen. It has a special body
on the chassis (frame) of a
Volkswagen Beetle. Like the
Beetle, it has a rear engine.

BALL BEARINGS

*You will need: A4 sheet of stiff card,
scissors, sticky tape, five 1cm x 20cm
strips of corrugated card,
16 glass marbles.*

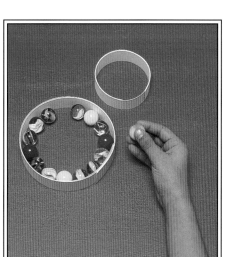

1 Cut two strips of stiff card, both
1.5cm wide. The first one
should be 20cm long and the second
10cm long. Make both into circle
shapes. Tape the ends together.

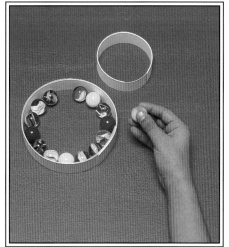

2 Use the strips of corrugated card
to line the inside of the larger
card circle. Put all five strips in,
and make sure that they are packed
very closely together.

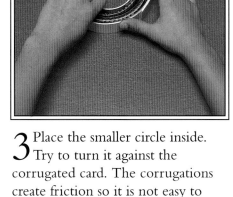

3 Place the smaller circle inside.
Try to turn it against the
corrugated card. The corrugations
create friction so it is not easy to
turn the smaller circle.

4 Take the smaller circle and the
corrugated strips out of the large
circle. Now line the inside of the
larger circle with the marbles until
there are no gaps between them.

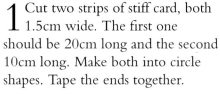

5 Place the smaller circle inside the
larger one again. Turn the small
circle. It moves very easily. The
smooth surface of the glass marbles
creates much less friction.

CLASSIC MODELS

DIFFERENT PEOPLE collect different kinds of cars. Those who are looking for style collect classic cars (at least 20 years old). Often the cars come from the 1950s, 1960s and 1970s. Owners take pride in the exceptional design and quality of the vehicles. For example, Rolls-Royces of any era look distinctive, and their engines and other mechanical parts were made with unusual care and the very best materials. High-performance classic sports cars such as the 1954 Mercedes-Benz Gullwing, the 1968 Aston Martin DB4, the 1960s Ford Mustang and the 1988 Porsche 959 are popular too.

Collectors of classic cars often belong to specialist clubs. The clubs help them to find the spare parts needed for their cars, and to meet people who are interested in the same models. Motor museums such as the Museum of Automobile History in the US, the National Motor Museum in the UK and the Porsche Museum in Germany exhibit classic cars for people to look at and enjoy.

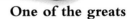

One of the greats
Few sports cars are as eagerly collected as the 1949 Jaguar XK120. It combines high speed with good looks. Its six-cylinder engine has double overhead camshafts (to control the valves in the cylinder heads). It can reach speeds of up to 193km/hour.

Bumper beauty
US car makers of the 1950s such as Cadillac created cars that shone with large areas of chrome (shiny metal). Bumpers and radiator grilles were moulded into streamlined shapes to catch the eye.

Up, up and away
The Mercedes-Benz 300SL sports car was built by hand, so only 1400 of them were ever made The car has one very striking feature. Its passenger and driver doors open upwards from the roof of the car. The unusual design gave the car its nickname 'The Gullwing', because the open doors look like a seagull. It is not very easy to get in and out of the car. Once inside, the driver and passenger sit close to the ground. The engine of the Gullwing was also set very low, to make sure that the driver could see over the top of the long bonnet.

Air-cooled cool
The 911 series Porsche Carrera was first made in 1964. The Porsche first appeared in 1939, as a higher-powered, streamlined, variation of the Volkswagen Beetle. Like the Beetle, the Porsche engine was air-cooled. Then, in 1997, the firm produced its first water-cooled car, the 928.

Classic car, classic film
The 1997 film comedy *Austin Powers* used many different examples of 1960s style. They all helped to recreate the fun-loving, swinging image of that period. In this scene, the hero of the film, played by Mike Myers, is standing up in the seat of a 1960s Jaguar E-Type. The bullet shape of this car is a classic design of the period.

FACT BOX

• The classic Jaguar E-type was Britain's fastest production-line car in 1961. Its top speed was 241km/hour.

• The 1968 Ferrari 365GTB4 Daytona is still one of the world's fastest cars. It has a top speed of 281km/hour.

• A 1926 Bentley 3-litre four-seat tourer was auctioned for £105,000 in 2000.

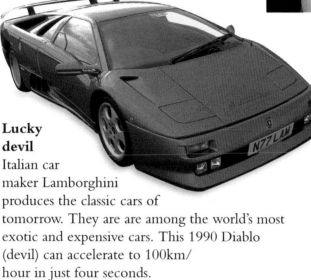

Lucky devil
Italian car maker Lamborghini produces the classic cars of tomorrow. They are are among the world's most exotic and expensive cars. This 1990 Diablo (devil) can accelerate to 100km/hour in just four seconds.

Classic performance
The British car maker Jaguar made many classic models in the past, such as the XK120 and the E-Type. The cars it makes today are also of top quality and performance. This 250km/hour XKR convertible's engine is supercharged to give extra power.

Super-streamlined
Modern sports-car maker Marcos designs cars such as the Mantis that are destined to become classics of the future. They have luxurious interiors and powerful engines to match any of the old greats. The streamlining on the front of this Mantis gives the car a look that stands out from other sports cars.

SPORTS CARS

SPORTS CARS, also known as roadsters, are made for speed, not comfort. Their engines are more powerful than those in everyday cars. In addition, they usually have only two seats. That way they carry less weight than ordinary cars. A French Delage super-sports car made an international record in 1932 with a speed of 180km/hour. In 1996, the British Lotus Esprit V8 arrived on the scene with a top speed of 274km/hour. Sports cars are driven on ordinary roads but they can also be driven in races. The 1972 Italian Lancia Stratos won the Monte Carlo Rally five times. The engines and bodies of sports cars are often developed from racing cars and have been tried out under tough conditions. The Le Mans 24-hour race in France is used as a gruelling testing ground for sports-car engines.

Breezing along
A 1904 Mercedes was no car to drive if you caught cold easily. There was no such thing as a convertible (a sports car with a folding roof) in 1904. Even so, this Mercedes was built for speed. A restored model shows the beautiful headlamps and coachwork (bodywork) created for this masterpiece of early car engineering.

Red roadster
This is a Big Healey, one of the larger models produced by the British car maker Austin Healey. The company are also known for their small sports car, the Sprite, nicknamed Frogeye because of its bulbous headlamps. Austin Healey ceased production in 1971, but their cars are favourites with collectors.

FACT BOX

• Jaguar produced their first sports car, the SS90, in 1935.

• The 1968 Aston Martin DB5 was the favourite car of James Bond.

• The Chevrolet Camaro was first produced in 1967 and is a powerful sports car, still popular today among collectors. The 1989 model had a V-8 engine that could reach 240km/hour.

• The MG sports cars are so-called because the company that made them was originally called Morris Garages.

Red bullet
The 1961 Jaguar E-Type's engine was developed from the one used in Jaguar's D-Type racing cars. Jaguar regularly took part in racing car events in the 1950s. The D-Type was a truly great racing car. It won the Le Mans 24-hour race four times between 1953 and 1957.

Pushy Porsche

The rear wing sticking out of the back of the Porsche 911 Turbo improves the flow of air over the back of the car when it travels at speed. It works by flattening out the air flow as it moves over the top of the car and down the rear. This helps to keep the car's body firmly on the road and the driver in control on tight bends.

Cool bug

The Volkswagen Beetle was always seen as a cheap family car. Then the 1968 Cabriolet appeared and surprised everyone. Volkswagen had made the engine more powerful to bring it into the same speed range as other small sports cars. It also had a flexible hood that could roll back in hot weather. Cars like this are called convertibles. This sporty Beetle is one of many changes the design has gone through since it was first produced in 1939.

Silver speeder

The Bugatti company started building high-quality sports and racing cars in 1909, first in Germany and then in France. When the firm was sold in 1956, people feared it would never make cars again. In 1991, however, the Bugatti EB110 appeared, hoping to keep the glory of the past alive. Its design, 12-valve engine and four-wheel drive were praised widely. In 1994, Bugatti closed again, but the company was later bought by Volkswagen.

Classy convertible

The BMW (*Bayerische Motoren Werke*) company has made cars and motorcycles in the German city of Munich since 1928. In the 1970s, they began to sell more of their cars outside Germany. By the 1980s, BMWs were popular throughout the world. Although this 3-series convertible from the 1990s has four seats, its 190km/hour top speed means it is still seen as a two-door sports car.

SUSPENSION

The earliest cars used coach wheels made of wood and metal. They gave a very bumpy ride. In the early 1900s, the French company Michelin made a rubber tyre with an inflatable inner tube. The idea came from the inner tube tyre that John Dunlop developed in the late 1800s for bicycles. The outer part of the tyre was made of rubber. Inside it had a tube filled with air. The air cushioned the car's contact with the road and driving became much more comfortable.

All car tyres had inner tubes until the 1950s. From then on, more tubeless tyres were made. In these, air is held in a web of wire and an inner tyre that fits tightly on the wheel rim. Cars use suspension systems, as well as air-filled tyres, as cushioning. Suspension systems are attached to a car's wheels to absorb impacts from the road. In modern cars, these are usually either coiled springs, shaped rubber cones or gas-filled cylinders.

Thick and thin
The engines on hot rods (cars with boosted engines) drive the rear wheels. These wheels often have thick tyres. This means there is a lot of contact between the road surface and the tyre surface, helping the car to grip the road when accelerating.

Suspension
A car's suspension system makes driving comfortable. It prevents the car from being bumped up and down too much on bumpy roads. In the early 1900s, car suspension was the same as the suspension in horse-drawn carriages. Modern cars use much more sophisticated systems. The Jaguar XKR Coupe shown here has a coiled spring system.

The suspension system is attached to each wheel. If the car goes over a 5cm bump, the wheel will go up 5cm too, but the car's body will move up less distance. The suspension system absorbs the impact. After going over the bump, the car's body will sink down slowly, too. Hydraulic cylinders (cylinders full of a liquid, such as oil, or gas) do this. The cylinders are called dampers, because they damp down the effect of the bump.

Taking off

Rally cars travel so quickly that when they come over the top of a hill they can leave the ground for a second or two. Then they come back down to earth with a stomach-churning bump. A hard landing can shatter a car's axles and put the car out of the competition. Rally cars take this kind of punishment hour after hour, day after day. They have to be fitted with extra-tough suspension systems.

Early tyres

A 1903 Mercedes-Benz sports car is fitted with tyres which have a rubber outer casing. Inside these were rubber tubesfilled with air, just like the inner tubes in bicycle tyres. Tyre manufacturers stopped including inner tubes in car tyres from the 1950s onwards. Drivers were having too many punctures.

Extreme machine

Four lorry wheels have hijacked a pickup truck to provide a well-cushioned ride. In the quest for ever more bizarre effects, someone has put a pickup truck on top of a metal frame. The frame is then specially linked to the type of tyres normally seen on enormous road vehicles such as earth-moving lorries. Suspension on this scale allows the truck to travel over extremely uneven surfaces, such as a stony quarry floor.

Big smoothie

Limousines look spectacular and provide exceptional levels of comfort. Stretch limousines are the most luxurious of all. They are often used for weddings and other important events. Very long cars like this have what is known as SRC (Selective Ride Control) suspension to make for an extra-smooth ride. Computers control chambers filled with gas that is pressurized by a pump. The compressed air absorbs shocks from the road.

HOME FROM HOME

THE GREAT advantage of setting off on an adventure by car is that you can go where you want, when you want. It is even possible to travel to places where there may be no towns or people. Once you're there, however, what do you do when you want to go to sleep at night? One solution is to drive a special car such as a multi-purpose vehicle (MPV) or a recreational vehicle (RV). They are built to provide sleeping space. Smaller ones have car seats that will lie flat to make a bed. Larger RVs have cabins with built-in bunks, kitchens and sitting areas. They may also have televisions, music systems, microwave ovens and all the high-tech equipment that can be found in a conventional house. The interiors of top-of-the-range RVs can be built according to the buyer's preferences.

Long way from home

Long-distance truck drivers, who drive thousands of kilometres every year, often travel through regions where there are very few towns or villages. At night the driver finds a safe place to park, then sleeps in a built-in bunk on a shelf behind the driver's seat.

Time for a drink

Rolls-Royce built the 1960 Phantom as a touring car for people who wanted to travel to the countryside and eat when they arrived. The small seats fold down when the car is moving and pull up in front of the drinks cabinet when the car is stopped. Cars such as this were often driven to outdoor events such as horse race meetings, where eating a picnic from a car is a tradition.

Open-air life

Caravans are mobile living units that can be towed from place to place by cars. Towing a caravan requires a lot of extra power from the car, so larger vehicles are the most suitable. Drivers have to keep their speed down when pulling a caravan, because the caravan could easily flip over.

SCENTED CAR REFRESHER

You will need: *200ml water, mixing bowl, 200g plain flour, wooden spoon, baking tray, pencil, bottle of essential oil, paintbrush, four colours of acrylic paint, 45cm length of string.*

1 Pour the water into a mixing bowl. Stir in the flour slowly with a wooden spoon. Continue to stir until the paste thickens into a dough mixture that you can mould.

2 Place the dough mixture in the baking tray. Mould the dough into a bell shape that bulges out at the bottom. Roughly shape a roof at the top and wheels underneath.

3 Wet the rough shape so it is easy to mould a design on it. Smooth your fingers over the top area to make a windscreen. Shape the wheels more accurately.

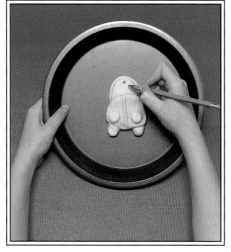

4 Make small holes in the car and one larger hole in the top. Sprinkle essential oil in the holes. Bake in an oven for 45 minutes at 150°C (Gas Mark 2).

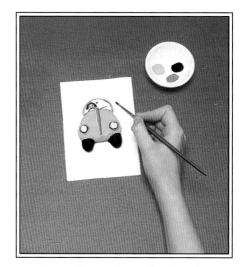

5 Once the car is cool, place it on a sheet of paper. Paint the bonnet first, then the details, such as a driver's face. Add lines around the headlights.

6 Allow the paint to dry. Thread the piece of string through the hole in the top of the car's windscreen. Double the string back and knot it to make a noose.

7 Your air freshener is all ready to go in a real car. Now you can put it on the dashboard, hang it from the back of a seat or put it on the shelf in front of the rear window. It will make any car smell fresh and clean.

FUEL CONSUMPTION

The amount of petrol a car uses depends on the weight of the car, the speed it is travelling and the size and efficiency of the engine. Pressing on the accelerator pedal lets more fuel flow into the engine's cylinders, speeding the car up. Most ordinary cars have four cylinders. A few extremely economical cars have two cylinders, and some powerful sports cars have six or even eight. Today, cars of all engine size are designed to use as little petrol as possible. This is because the oil from which petrol is made is much more expensive than it was in the 1950s and 1960s. The average modern car can travel 15km or 20km on one litre of petrol. Gas (petrol) guzzlers such as the US Cadillac Fleetwood could only drive 4km on a litre of petrol.

Roaring oldie
Super Street hot rodders often take the bodies of old cars and combine them with modern parts. The 1950s car body here has been joined to big tyres by a complicated suspension system. Some hot rodders use special chemical fuels such as ethanol and nitromethane. When they burn, they get much hotter than petrol. The extra heat helps them to accelerate to very high speeds.

FACT BOX

• Rising oil prices in the late 1900s led to the creation of gasohol, a mixture of lead-free petrol and ethanol. Ethanol can be made from plants such as grain and potatoes.

• Traces of the metal lead in car exhaust fumes are harmful to health. It is thought that many people suffered lead poisoning. Now, lead-free petrol has been developed and is widely available.

Where's the car?
Members of the Eddie Jordan pitstop crew swarm over the Jordan 199 at the Australian Grand Prix in 1999. In the centre, a team member holds the hose that forces fuel into the car's petrol tank at high pressure. Up to 100 litres of fuel can be pumped into the car in about 10 seconds. Speed is essential. Every second in the pit lane is equal to about 60m lost on the track.

Two-carb Caddy

The Cadillacs of the 1950s are reminders of a time when petrol was cheap and car makers could make big, heavy cars. In the 1970s, the price of oil rose dramatically, so petrol became much more expensive. The 1955 Cadillac Fleetwood had two carburettors, even though most cars built at that time would have had just one. The second carburettor was needed because the Fleetwood used so much petrol.

Pink thunderbird

The sleek rear fins and supercool spare-wheel casing made the 1957 Ford Thunderbird a car that people remembered long after Ford stopped making the model. This restored T-Bird is fitted out as a convertible. When the cars were first sold, buyers were given both a hard top and a convertible top. They could fit whichever one they wanted. In 1998, the 1957 Thunderbird's good looks earned it a Lifetime Automotive Design Achievement Award from the Detroit Institute of Ophthalmology in the USA.

Twice as much

Cars that use a lot of petrol may have two or even four exhausts. Twin exhausts extract waste gases from the engine in a more efficient way than a single exhaust could, which allows the engine to perform more efficiently too.

Flying flatbed

Flatbeds (open trucks) such as this are favourites for customising enthusiasts. They take an old truck and turn it into an ORV (Off-Road Vehicle). An ORV consumes lots of petrol as it drives across rough conditions, often far from any petrol stations. They carry large reservoir cans of petrol in case they run out.

SPEED RECORDS

IN MORE than a hundred years of car building, cars have reached faster and faster speeds. In 1899, the Belgian inventor Camille Jenatzy was the first person to drive a car faster than 100km/hour. The car, designed by Jenatzy himself, ran on electricity. In the same year, Sir Charles Wakefield created his Castrol Motor Oil company. The company awards the official trophy for the land-speed record to drivers who break the record. The trophy was first won in 1914 by the Englishman L.G. Hornsted. He reached a speed of 200km/hour in a car from the German car maker Benz. Since then 38 other people have broken the record. The last person to succeed was the RAF Tornado pilot Andy Green, on 13 October 1997. His car, powered by two jet engines, broke the sound barrier (sound travels at a speed of 1,226km/hour), reaching 1,228km/hour.

Satisfaction at last

Between December 1898 and April 1899, there were no less than six attempts to beat the land-speed record. All of them were made by drivers in electric cars. The fastest, in April, was the Belgian Camille Jenatzy who reached 106km/hour. He called his car *La Jamais Contente* (Never Satisfied) because he had already tried to set the land-speed record twice before.

Gas-powered wheels

Finding a long, flat, hard surface to travel on is very important when trying to set a speed record on land. Donald Campbell thundered across the Lake Eyre Salt Flats in Australia in 1964. He reached a speed of 649km/hour in his gas-turbine powered car Bluebird. He was following in the footsteps of his father Malcolm, who set nine land-speed records.

Golden goer

The Golden Arrow set a land-speed record of 370km/hour on 11 March 1929. The enormous, streamlined car was powered by a Napier-Lion aeroplane engine. It flashed along the hard, white sand at Daytona Beach in Florida, USA. The driver was Major Henry Seagrave. After setting the land-speed record, Seagrave went on to set the world water-speed record.

FACT BOX

• The 160-square km salt flats at Bonneville in the US state of Utah were the setting for 18 land-speed records between the years 1935 and 1970.

• The 'Flying Mile' at the Brooklands racing track in Britain was the scene of the first two land-speed records.

• The US drag racer Art Arfons set the land-speed record three times. He reached 698km/hour on 5 October 1964. Just 22 days later he drove at 863km/hour. One year later he travelled at 927km/hour.

Goodbye, Mr Bond

In the 1974 Bond film *The Man with the Golden Gun*, the character James Bond performs many death-defying feats. His car takes at least as much punishment as the Secret Service Agent himself. To fly across the river, the car would have had to be travelling at 200km/hour when taking off from the ramp.

Expensive record

The Black Rock Desert in Nevada, USA was the scene for another record-breaking attempt in 1983. On this dried lake bed, in blistering desert heat, Richard Noble set a new record of 1,018km/hour. He was driving the specially made jet-engine powered Thrust 2. Making a speed record attempt costs a lot of money. The advertisements plastered all over the car are for businesses that donated money for this record attempt.

Supersonic car

In 1997 Andy Green drove the Thrust SSC at an incredible 1,228km/hour. He did not just set a new world land-speed record, he travelled faster than the speed of sound (1,226km/hour). Until then, speeds greater than that of sound had only been possible in flight. Andy was used to the speed because he was a jet pilot for the British Royal Air Force.

Head for the horizon

Ever since commercial films started to be made in the early 1900s, car chases have formed part of the action. The cars are usually driven by stunt men and women specially trained in fast driving. In the 1991 film *Thelma and Louise*, the two heroines are chased by dozens of police cars. In the end, the two women drive over the edge of a cliff.

ROADS AND MOTORWAYS

BEFORE THE 1800s, most roads were just earth tracks. Some roads in cities and towns were made of stone and wood blocks, which gave a rough ride. Macadam roads (roads covered in a hard layer of tiny stones) were a great improvement in the 1800s, but with the invention of cars at the end of the 1800s, new road surfaces were needed. Roads made of asphalt (a mixture of bitumen and stone) and concrete offered the hardness and smoothness that cars needed to travel safely and quickly.

The first motorway was completed in 1932 in Germany, between Cologne and Bonn. As car ownership grew during the second half of the 1900s, road building programmes followed. Some people think there are too many roads. They protest against the building of more roads because they want to protect the countryside.

Multi-lane moves
Motorways are called freeways in the USA. Car ownership and use has grown relentlessly, and the freeways have grown too. In the last 30 years the freeways have increased in size from four lanes to 12 lanes, and even to 16 lanes on some stretches.

Pay as you go
The enormous costs of building motorways can be partly paid for by charging drivers a toll (payment for using a road) when they travel on the new roads. The road owners set up barriers through which a car must pass to drive on to the road. Drivers crossing the Queen Elizabeth Bridge in Dartford, England stop at toll booths to buy tickets that allow them to drive over the bridge.

Keep calm
Traffic calming is the name given to the different ways of slowing down traffic speed. Building speed humps (bumps in the road) is one example of traffic calming. The speed humps force drivers to slow down in areas where there is a lot of housing. Slower car speeds help to prevent accidents.

Going places

Modern countries need well-built roads so that goods and people can travel easily between cities and towns. This is Interstate 35 approaching the US city of Minneapolis. It is part of the vast interstate highway system that links the entire USA.

Major to minor

Road networks are often much easier to understand from the air. A looped road links two major highways. Long curving roads such as these allow drivers to switch between major roads without having to stop at a junction. The roads that link up major roads are called sliproads.

Night guide

Small glass reflectors called Catseyes help drivers to see the road at night. The Catseyes are set at regular intervals in the middle of the road. They gleam brightly when a car's headlights shine on them. The British inventor Percy Shaw invented the device in 1933, after noticing how a cat's eyes shine at night.

The long and winding road

There are still many narrow old roads in remote areas. They twist and turn for kilometres through beautiful countryside. There is much less traffic on country roads, and they offer an enjoyable test of driving skills. Four-wheel drive vehicles handle particularly well on the tight corners and steep slopes.

Roadworks ahead

Modern roads carry a lot of traffic and need constant repair and maintenance. They cannot simply be shut down while that happens. Instead, some lanes are closed for repair while others remain open. The long lines of plastic cones on this stretch of motorway have restricted traffic to one lane on one side and two lanes on the other side.

BADGES AND MASCOTS

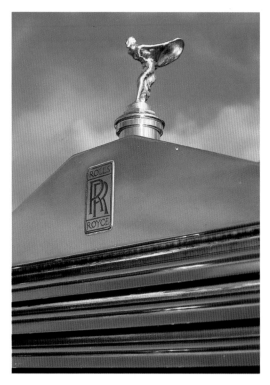

CAR MANUFACTURERS take pride in the work that goes into the machines that they make. They put badges or symbols on their cars to show which company made the car. The badges are usually found on the car bonnet, where they are easy to spot. There are many different car makers all over the world, and they each make a different badge. The instantly recognizable designs of the most prestigious companies, such as the Silver Lady on Rolls-Royces or the three-spoked circle on Mercedes cars, suggest elegance or power. Other celebrated symbols are the rearing horse on the front of cars made by the Italian Ferrari company, and the VW symbol used on Volkswagen cars. Sometimes these badges are called mascots, perhaps because car makers see them as a symbol of good luck. When people identify a car's badge, they immediately know the name of the car maker. In this project, you can make your own car mascot to symbolize the kind of car you like.

Leading lady

All Rolls-Royce cars carry a winged figure mascot on the bonnet. It is called The Spirit of Ecstasy and was created by the sculptor Charles Sykes. The figure first appeared on Rolls-Royce cars in 1911. In modern Rolls-Royces, the mascot folds down backwards into the bonnet during an accident to avoid injury.

BONNET BEAUTY

You will need: *A4 sheet of cardboard, pencil, scissors, adhesive tape, bradawl, glue, matchstick, newspaper, fork, 250g flour, 200ml water, tin of silver aerosol paint, fine paintbrush, black paint.*

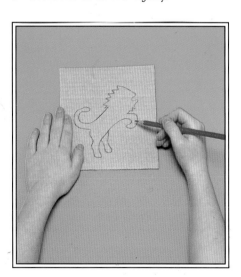

1 Cut a piece measuring 15 x 20cm from the cardboard. Use a pencil to draw the outline of the shape you want to put on your car bonnet on the cardboard sheet.

2 Use the scissors to cut roughly around the badge shape. Then cut around the outline accurately. Be careful not to cut off any of the detail in your drawing.

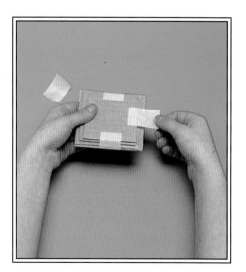

3 Cut three square pieces from the cardboard, one 5cm, one 6cm and one 7cm. Tape the smallest on top of the next largest and those on top of the largest as a solid base.

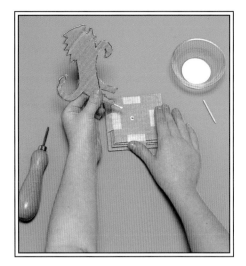

4 Make a hole in the centre of the base with the bradawl. Put a glued matchstick in the bottom of your badge. Insert it into the hole in the base so that the badge stands upright.

5 Tear strips of newspaper. Mix flour and water with a fork, to make a thick paste. Dip the paper in the mixture. Apply the wet paper to the badge in three layers.

6 When the newspaper is dry, spray your badge with aerosol paint. Be careful to point the can downwards, away from you. Put a piece of paper under the badge.

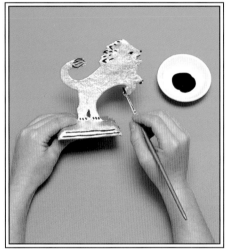

7 Use the paintbrush to apply black lines on the badge where you want to show more detail. For example this one shows detail of the lion's mane, tail and paws.

Speeder's shield

The badge on Porsche cars is like a coat of arms from medieval times. In the past, important people made decorations on shield shapes to tell others who their ancestors were and where they came from.

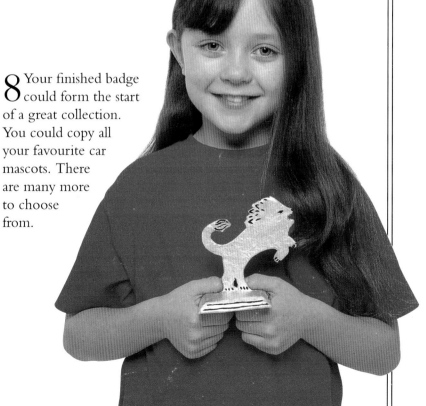

8 Your finished badge could form the start of a great collection. You could copy all your favourite car mascots. There are many more to choose from.

Roar of power

Jaguar cars have used the model of the leaping jaguar as their mascot for many years. More recent models do not have the statuette on the bonnet. They have been declared illegal because they could cause injury to pedestrians in an accident.

THE FUTURE

THE CARS of the future already exist, but only as the still-secret designs of car makers. The use of in-car computers will be one of the main ways in which cars will change. These already control engine performance, navigation aids and air temperature. In future, a computer chip may apply the brakes automatically when the car in front is too close, or flash up HUDs (Head Up Display) messages on the windscreen about road conditions ahead.

Designers and engineers will continue to develop fuel-efficient cars (ones that use as little petrol as possible), such as the Toyota Echo. They will also look at the potential of alternative power sources such as electricity, natural gas (a gas found under the ground), solar power (power from the sun's energy) and hydrogen (a gas in the earth's atmosphere). Of all the many developments that will occur, one is almost certain. There will be even more cars on the roads.

Hot item
Cars powered by energy from the sun (solar power) would be better for the environment than petrol engine cars. Photo-electric cells on the back of the car turn energy from the sun's rays into electricity. This energy is stored in batteries inside the car. The batteries then supply power to the engine. At the moment this method can only store enough energy to power small cars. Scientists are trying to find a way to use solar power in bigger vehicles.

FACT BOX

• The US car manufacturer General Motors is developing a car that will change its shape from a saloon car to a pickup truck by means of voice-activated commands spoken by the driver in the front seat.

• Car makers are building concept (future idea) cars in which each seat has its own LCD (liquid-crystal display) screen. Passengers will be able to send and receive e-mail, browse the internet, make phone calls and read maps.

Take me home
GPS (Global Positioning System) navigation aids are already fitted into top-range cars. A radio aerial in the car sends a signal to one of the 24 GPS satellites that orbit the earth. The satellite sends a signal back to the car giving its exact position on the earth. The data is sent to a computer that reads maps stored on a CD-ROM. A small screen on the dashboard of the car displays a map of the road network and the position of the car on the map. If the driver inputs the destination, the screen displays the best route.

Neat package

Car makers produced classic microcars such as the BMW Isetta in the 1950s and 1960s. In the future, they will continue to make very small cars. They are ideal for short journeys in built-up areas. The number of cars in towns and cities continues to grow. Extra-small vehicles such as the Smart car could be the answer to parking problems. It is so short (2.5m) that it can park not just along the edge of the road, but front-on with the pavement.

Snappy mover

Research has shown that on most journeys, the average number of people who travel in a car is two. Car makers now know that two-seater cars like the one shown here make a lot of sense for many drivers. Less metal is needed to make them, they use less fuel, and they are cheaper to buy. A car as small as this is also much easier to manoeuvre in the tight spaces of modern cities.

Three-wheel dream

One-person cars seem an obvious answer to many traffic problems. They are not always a hit with drivers, however. The British inventor Sir Clive Sinclair produced the electric-powered Sinclair C5 in 1985. The vehicle was not very popular, and was soon taken out of production.

Future taxi

Will the four-wheel yellow cabs of New York today be replaced by three-wheel taxis in the future? The 1992 science-fiction film *Freejack* showed great imagination in guessing what the taxicabs of tomorrow might look like.

TRAIN & TRACK

RUNNING ON RAILS

Throughout history, people have looked for ways to move themselves and their possessions faster and more efficiently. Wheels were invented about 5,500 years ago. As wheels are round, they turn well on smooth surfaces and reduce the rubbing, slowing force called friction. However, it soon became clear that wheels do not work well on rough, soft or muddy ground.

To solve this problem, tracks of wood or stone were cut into or laid on to the ground to provide a smooth surface on which wheels could turn. This kept friction to a minimum, so that vehicles could move more easily and shift heavier loads.

The ancient Greeks made the first railed tracks in about 400BC by cutting grooved rails into rock. They hauled ships overland by setting them on wheeled trolleys that ran along the tracks. Iron rails came into use in Europe by the mid-1700s. They were laid, mainly in mines, to transport wagons loaded with coal or metal ores. Steam-powered locomotives were developed in the early 1800s. Before then, wagons in mines were pulled by horses or by the miners themselves, which was slow and only possible for short distances.

Pulling power

A horse pulls a freight wagon along rails. Modern railways developed from ones first laid in European mines in the mid-1500s. Heavy loads, such as coal and metal ore, were carried in wagons with wheels that ran along wooden planks. The wagons were guided by a peg under the wagon, which slotted into a gap between the planks. Horses and sometimes even human labourers were used to haul the wagons long before steam locomotives were invented.

Riding rails

It is just possible to make out the grooves where iron rails were laid at the Penydarran Ironworks in South Wales in the early 1800s. The world's first steam-powered train ran along these rails on 13 February 1804. The locomotive was designed by British engineer Richard Trevithick and hauled wagons 14.5km at a speed of 8km/h.

1769–1810	1811–1830	1831–1860	1861–1880
1769 Frenchman Nicholas Cugnot builds the first steam-powered vehicle.	**1825** The Stockton and Darlington Railway opens in Britain – the first public railway to use steam-powered locomotives.	**1833** George Stephenson devises the steam brake cylinder to operate brake blocks on the driving wheels of steam locomotives.	**1863** London Underground's Metropolitan Line opens and is the world's first underground passenger railway.
	1827 The Baltimore and Ohio Railroad is chartered to run from Baltimore to the River Ohio, Virginia, in the USA.		**1864** American George Pullman builds the first sleeping car, the *Pioneer.*
			1868 Pullman builds the first dining car.
1804 British Engineer Richard Trevithick tests the first steam locomotive for the Penydarran Ironworks in Wales.	**1829** Robert and George Stephenson's *Rocket* wins the Rainhill Trials. It becomes the locomotive used for the Liverpool and Manchester Railway.		**1869** The Central Pacific and Union Pacific railroads meet at Promontory Summit, linking the east and west coasts of the USA.
1808 Trevithick builds a circular railway in London, Britain, and exhibits the *Catch Me Who Can* locomotive.		**1840s** Semaphore signalling is introduced. First tickets for train journeys are issued.	**1872** American George Westinghouse patents an automatic air-braking system.

Trackless trains

The world's longest trackless train runs at Lake County Museum in Columbia, South Carolina, in the USA. Trackless trains are common in theme parks. They carry passengers in carts or wagons running on rubber-tyred wheels. The trains are pulled by a tractor that is made to look like a railway locomotive.

Puffing Billy

The locomotive in this painting was nicknamed *Puffing Billy* because it was one of the earliest to have a chimney. It was designed by British mine engineer William Hedley and built in 1813. The first steam engines were built in the early 1700s. They were used to pump water from mineshafts, not to power vehicles. *Puffing Billy* can be seen today in the Science Museum in London, Britain. It is the world's oldest surviving steam locomotive.

Modern rail networks

Today nearly all countries in the world have their own railway network. Thousands of kilometres of track criss-cross the continents. Steam power has now given way to newer inventions. Most modern trains are hauled by locomotives powered by diesel engines, by electricity drawn from overhead cables or from an electrified third rail on the track.

1881–1900

1883 THE LUXURIOUS *ORIENT-EXPRESS* first runs on 5 June from Paris, France, to Bucharest in Romania.

1893 THE NEW YORK CENTRAL AND HUDSON River Railroad claims that its steam locomotive *No. 999* travels faster than 100mph, or 160km/h.

1895 BALTIMORE AND OHIO *No. 1* is the first electric locomotive to run on the mainline Baltimore and Ohio Railroad.

1900 THE PARIS *METRO* opens.

1901–1950

1901 THE FIRST COMMERCIAL monorail opens in Wuppertal, northwestern Germany.

1904 THE NEW YORK CITY subway opens.

1938 *MALLARD* SETS the world speed record for a steam-powered locomotive (203km/h).

1940s UNION PACIFIC BIG BOYS are built by the American Locomotive Company.

1951–1980

1955 THE WORLD'S MOST POWERFUL single-unit diesel-electric locomotives, the Deltics, first run between London and Liverpool.

1957 TRANS-EUROP EXPRESS (TEE) fleet of trains operates an international rail service across western Europe.

1964 THE BULLET TRAIN first runs on the Tokaido Shinkansen between Tokyo and Osaka in Japan.

1980 THE FIRST MAGLEV (magnetic levitation) service opens at Birmingham Airport.

1981–present

1981 TGV (*TRAIN À GRANDE VITESSE*) first runs between Paris and Lyon in France.

1994 CHANNEL TUNNEL completed, linking rail networks in Britain and the Continent.

1996 MAGLEV TRAIN ON THE Yamanashi test line in Japan reaches a staggering 560km/h.

RAILWAY TRACK

A FULLY LADEN freight or passenger train is heavy, so the track it runs on has to be tough. Nowadays, rails are made from steel, which is a much stronger material than the cast iron used for the first railways. The shape of the rail also helps to make it tough. If you sliced through a rail from top to bottom you would see it has an 'I'-shaped cross section. The broad, flat bottom narrows into the 'waist' of the I and widens again into a curved head. Most countries use a rail shaped like this.

Tracks are made up of lengths of rail, which are laid on wooden or concrete crossbeams called sleepers. Train wheels are a set distance apart, so rails must be a set distance apart, too. The distance between rails is called the gauge. In Britain, the gauge was fixed at 1.435m (4ft 8½in) in the mid-1800s. Before then, the width of trains and gauges varied from one rail network to the next. So a train from one rail network could not run over the lines of another rail network.

Hard labour

Laying rail track is backbreaking work. Up until the mid-1900s, it was always done by hand. The ground is levelled first. Then crushed rock is laid to form a solid base before the sleepers are put into position. The rails rest on metal baseplates to hold them firm. The baseplates are secured to the sleepers either by spikes (big nails), track bolts or large metal spring-clips. Today, machines are used to lay track in most countries, although some countries still use manual labour.

MAKING TRACKS

You will need: *two sheets of stiff card measuring 26 x 11cm, pencil, ruler, scissors, glue and glue brush, silver and brown paint, paintbrush, water pot, one sheet of foam board measuring 20 x 13cm, one sheet of A4 paper, masking tape, one sheet of thin card measuring 10 x 5cm.*

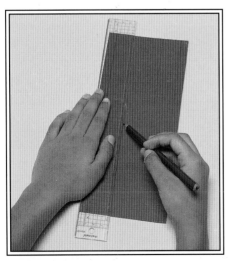

1 Place one 26 x 11cm piece of card lengthways. Draw a line 1cm in from each of the outside edges. Draw two more lines, each 3.5cm in from the outside edges. This is side A.

2 Turn the card over (side B) and place it lengthways. Measure and draw lines 4cm and 4.75cm in from each edge. Repeat steps 1 and 2 with the second piece of 26 x 11cm card.

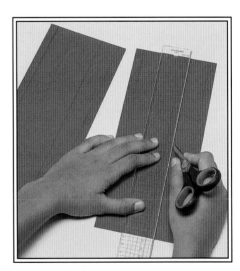

3 Hold the ruler firmly against one of the lines you have drawn. Use the tip of a pair of scissors to score along the line. Repeat for all lines on both sides of both pieces of card.

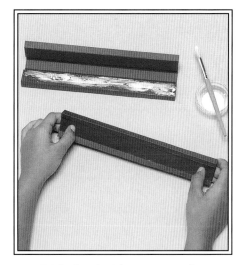

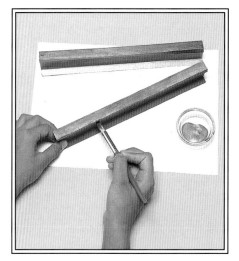

4 Place the cards A side up. For each one in turn, fold firmly along the two pairs of outer lines. Fold up from the scored side. Turn the card over. Repeat for inner lines.

5 With the A side up, press the folds into the I-shape of the rail. Open out again. Glue the B side of the 2cm-wide middle section as shown. Repeat for the second rail.

6 Give your two rails a metallic look by painting the upper (A) sides silver. Leave the paint to dry, then apply a second coat. Leave the second coat to dry.

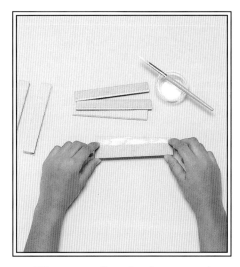

7 Use a pencil and ruler to mark out ten 13 x 2cm strips on the foam board. Cut them out. Glue two strips together to make five thick railway sleepers. Leave them to dry.

8 Paint the sleepers brown on their tops and sides to make them look like wood. Leave them to dry, then apply a second coat of paint. Leave the second coat to dry, too.

9 Lay the sleepers on a piece of paper, 3cm apart. Run a strip of masking tape down the middle to hold them in place.

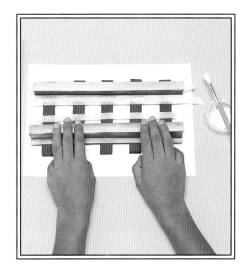

10 Glue the base of one rail and press it into place along the line of sleepers. The outside edge of the rail should be 1.5cm in from the edge of the sleeper. Glue the other track into position in the same way. Secure the rails in place with masking tape until the glue is dry. Then gently remove all masking tape.

11 Make at least two sets of rails. These will be able to carry the *Toy Train* and *Brake Van* described in later projects. To join the rails together, roll up the 10 x 5cm length of thin card. Insert one end into the top of the I-shape in one rail. Gently push the second rail on to the other end.

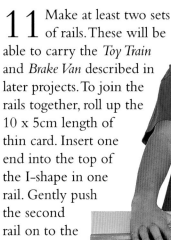

STEAMING AHEAD

Horses, oxen or people provided the pulling power for wagons on rails and roads for thousands of years. In the 1800s, inventors came up with an alternative. They worked out how to use steam power for pulling wheeled vehicles. In 1825, the world's first public steam railway, the 40km-long Stockton and Darlington line, opened in England. On its opening day, the train hauled both freight and passenger wagons. Later, it was used mainly for carrying coal.

Five years later, the Liverpool and Manchester line opened with its new, steam-driven passenger trains. The company had run a competition called the Rainhill Trials to find the best locomotive for its railway. Both horse-drawn and steam locomotives took part. The steam-driven *Rocket* won.

The success of the *Rocket* convinced investors to back the development of steam-powered locomotives. The brains behind the *Rocket* and the Stockton and Darlington and Liverpool and Manchester railways were George Stephenson and his son Robert. In 1823, they set up the world's first locomotive factory. Other British engineers began to experiment with steam power, and locomotives were made for use in Britain and around the world.

Race to success

The *Rocket,* designed and built by George and Robert Stephenson, convinced people that steam power was better than horse power. At the Rainhill Trials in 1829, the *Rocket* travelled 112km at an average speed of 24km/h.

Slow train to China

This Chinese locomotive is a KD class, which followed an American design. The Chinese did not make their own locomotives until they began to set up their own factories in the 1950s. Before then, locomotives had been imported from countries such as the USA, Britain and Japan. Some Chinese trains are still steam-driven today, although diesel and electric are rapidly replacing them.

hot gases pass through to boiler

firebox

cab

regulator valve

boiler tubes surrounded by water

engine

steam passes through pipes into cylinders

chimney

smokebox

steam valve

piston inside cylinder

driving wheels

coupling rod

connecting rod

leading wheels

Steam traction

A steam engine converts the energy released from combustion into kinetic energy or movement. First, fuel (most often coal) is burned in a firebox to produce hot gases. The gases pass through boiler tubes that run the length of the water-filled boiler. The hot, gas-filled tubes heat the surrounding water and turn it into steam. This steam passes into cylinders, each of which contains a close-fitting piston. The steam pushes the piston along. The steam then escapes via a valve (one-way opening), and the piston can move back again. Rods connect the piston to the wheels. As the piston moves back and forth, it moves the rods, which, in turn, make the wheels go round.

FACT BOX
• Steam locomotives need about 100 litres of water for every 1.6km they travel. It takes 12–25kg of coal – equivalent to seven or eight times the weight of the water – to turn the water into steam.

Big wheels

The Stirling Single locomotive had only one pair of large driving wheels (third in from the left). The driving wheels are driven directly by the piston and connecting rod from the cylinder. Most steam locomotives had two or more pairs of driving wheels linked by coupling rods. The Single, designed by British engineer Patrick Stirling in the 1870s, reached speeds of 129km/h.

The Big Boys

In the 1940s, American engineers were designing huge steam locomotives such as this Union Pacific Challenger. At more than 40m, the Union Pacific's Big Boys were the world's longest-ever steam locomotives – more than five times the length of the Stephensons' *Rocket*. They could haul long passenger or freight trains speedily across the USA's vast landscape.

BEARING THE LOAD

THE VEHICLE and machinery carried by a modern locomotive's underframe and wheels may weigh up to 100 tonnes. As bigger and more powerful locomotives were built, more wheels were added to carry the extra weight. Early steam locomotives such as the Stephensons' *Rocket* had only two pairs of wheels. Most steam locomotives had two, three or four pairs of driving wheels, all of which turn in response to power from the cylinders. The cylinders house the pistons, whose movement pushes the driving wheels around via a connecting rod.

The other wheels are connected to the driving wheel by a coupling rod, so that they turn at the same time. The small wheels in front of the driving wheels are called leading wheels. The ones behind are the trailing wheels. Locomotives are defined by the total number of wheels they have. For example, a 4-4-0 type locomotive has four leading, four driving and no trailing wheels.

Staying power

The coupling rod that connects the driving wheel to the other wheels is the lowest of the three rods in this picture. The connecting rod just above links the driving wheel with the cylinder. To stop train wheels from slipping sideways and falling off the rails, there is a rim called the flange on the inside of each wheel. This is a little different from the wheels you will make in this project, which have two flanges so that they sit snugly on the model rails from the *Making Tracks* project.

MAKING AN UNDERFRAME

You will need: *sheet of stiff card (size A2), pencil, ruler, pair of compasses, scissors, glue and glue brush, masking tape, four 10cm lengths of 0.5cm diameter dowel, four pieces of 5 x 5cm thin card, silver and black paint, paintbrush, water pot, four map pins.*

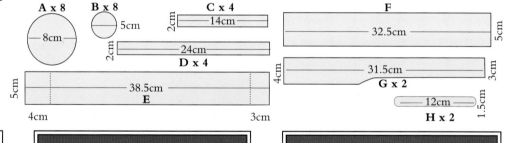

1 Draw and cut out the templates from the stiff card. Use a pair of compasses to draw the wheel templates A and B.

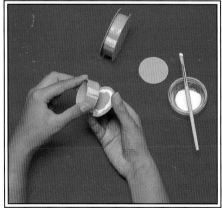

2 Roll the rim templates C and D into rings. Glue and tape to hold. Glue each small wheel circle on to either side of a small ring as shown. Repeat for big wheels. Leave to dry.

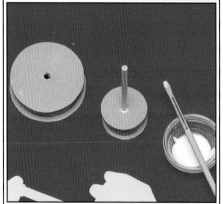

3 Use a pencil to enlarge the compass hole on one side of each wheel. Glue one end of each piece of dowel. Push the dowels into the holes of two big and two small wheels.

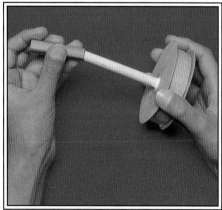

4 Roll the 5 x 5cm card into sleeves to fit loosely over each piece of dowel. Tape to hold. Make wheel pairs by fixing the remaining wheels on to the dowel as described in step 3.

5 When the glue is dry, paint all four pairs of wheels silver. You do not need to paint the dowel axles. Paint two coats, letting the first dry before you apply the second.

6 Use a ruler and pencil to mark eight equal segments on the outside of each wheel. Paint a small circle over the compass hole, and the centre of each segment black.

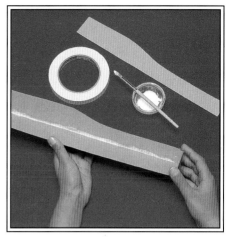

7 Fold along the dotted lines on E. Glue all three straight edges of template G and stick to template E. Repeat this for the other side. Secure all joins with masking tape.

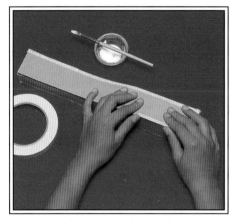

8 Glue the open edges of the underframe. Fit template F on top and hold until firm. Tape over the joins. Give the underframe two coats of black paint. Leave to dry.

9 Glue the card sleeves on to the base of the underframe. Small wheel axles go 3cm and 7cm from the front, big wheels 3.5cm and 13cm from the back. Tape to secure.

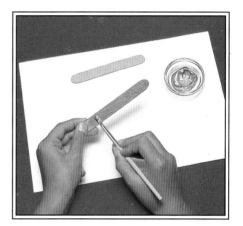

10 Give the coupling rods (H) two coats of silver paint. Let the paint dry between coats.

11 Press a map pin through each end of the coupling rods, about 0.5cm from edge. Carefully press the pin into each big wheel about 1.5cm beneath the centre.

12 The wheels on this underframe are arranged for a 4-4-0 type locomotive. You will be able to run the underframe along the model tracks you made in the *Making Tracks* project. The wheels will fit on the rails just like those of a real train. In real locomotives, however, the wheels are mounted on swivelling units called bogies. When the train comes to a curve in the track, the bogies move to allow the train to follow the curve. Each bogie has four to six wheels.

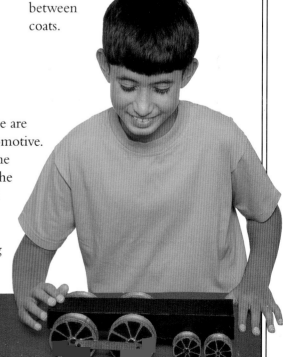

DIESEL AND ELECTRIC POWER

TODAY, MOST high-speed trains are either diesel, electric or a combination of the two. Diesel and electric trains are far more fuel-efficient, cost less to run and can stop or speed up more quickly than steam trains. Electric trains are also better for the environment, because they do not give off polluting exhaust fumes.

The first electric locomotive ran in 1879 at an exhibition in Berlin in Germany. However, it was another 20 or so years before railway companies began to introduce electric trains into regular service. Similarly, the first reliable diesel engine was demonstrated in 1889 by its inventor, the French-born German Rudolf Diesel. It took a further 25 years for railway engineers to design the first practical diesel locomotives. Diesel trains entered regular service during the 1920s in the USA, and during the 1930s in Britain. Steam locomotives were last used regularly in the USA in 1960, in 1968 in Britain and in 1977 in West Germany.

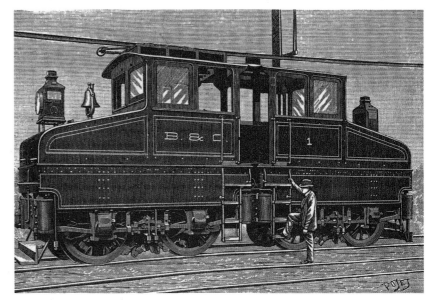

Electric pioneer
In 1895, the B&O *No. 1* became the world's first electric locomotive to run on a mainline railway. It entered service in Baltimore in the USA (B&O is short for Baltimore and Ohio Railroad). The route of the B&O *No. 1* took it through many tunnels. One of the advantages of electric locomotives is that, unlike steam trains, they do not fill tunnels and carriages with steam and smoke.

Beautiful Bugattis
Racing-car designer Ettore Bugatti designed this diesel train for the French *État* and Paris Lyons *Mediterranée* railways. In the early 1930s, Bugatti's first trains were diesel or petrol single railcars (self-propelled passenger carriages). Instead of being hauled by a locomotive, the railcar had its own engine. The railcar-and-carriage combination shown left was a later introduction. Bugatti came up with the train's streamlined shape by testing his designs in wind tunnels. In 1935, one of Bugatti's trains reached 196km/h, setting a world diesel train speed record.

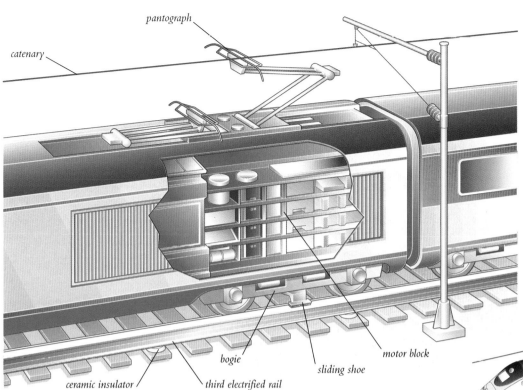

pantograph

catenary

bogie

motor block

sliding shoe

ceramic insulator

third electrified rail

Picking up power

Electric locomotives are powered in one of two ways. Some draw electricity from a catenary (overhead cable). This is connected to the locomotive by an 'arm' called a pantograph on the roof. Others draw power from a third rail. The locomotive connects to the rail by a device called a shoe. The Eurostar trains that operate in Europe can use either power source depending on what country they are travelling through.

Long-distance runner

Australian National Railways' diesel–electric engines work the long Indian Pacific route. This transcontinental railway runs between Perth, on the Indian Ocean, and Sydney, on the Pacific Ocean. These locomotives belong to the CL class that was introduced in 1970. This class was based on one that originated in the USA but was built in Sydney, Australia.

Dutch double decker

Dutch Railways' IRM (*InterRegio Materiel*) electric trains are double-decked to cater for high levels of traffic in the densely populated Netherlands. Passenger traffic is expected to increase rapidly, and so the Netherlands is investing heavily in its railways. Speeds on existing lines are limited to 140km/h, but new lines are being built for speeds of up to 220km/h.

Cisalpino Pendolino

Italy has developed a tilting train, or pendolino, called the ETR (*Elletro Treni Rapidi*) 470 Cisalpino. These dual-voltage trains are operated by an Italian-Swiss consortium (group of companies). Services began in September 1996 between Italy and Switzerland. The ETR 470 Cisalpino has been developed to be able to use existing rail networks at higher speeds by tilting into the curves as it travels. As a result, the top service speed of these trains is 250km/h.

MAPPING THE RAILWAYS

TRAINS CANNOT easily climb mountains or cope with sharp corners. Planning and mapping the route of a railway is not simply a matter of drawing a straight line between two destinations. New routes have to be worked out carefully, so that difficult terrain is avoided and time and money will not be wasted on tunnel- or bridge-building. Geographically accurate maps are made before work starts to show every bend of the planned railway and the height of the land it will run through. Once construction starts, separate teams of workers may be building sections of track in different parts of the country. The maps are essential to make sure they are all following the same route and will join up when the separate parts meet.

Passengers do not need such detailed maps. They just need to find out which train to catch to get to the place they want to go. They do not need to know each curve or bridge along the way, just the names of the stations. Passenger maps provide a simplified version of the railway routes, or sometimes a diagram.

Railroads in the Wild West
You can see how the railroads often followed a similar route to the wagon trails, passing through mountain passes or river valleys. After the first east-to-west-coast railroad was completed (the Central Pacific Railroad joined the Union Pacific Railroad in 1869), people could cross the continent in just ten days.

Early American railroad
A train runs along the Mohawk and Hudson Railroad, New York State, in the USA. This railway line opened in 1831 and was built to replace part of the 64km route of the Erie Canal. This section of the canal had several locks, which caused delays to the barges. The journey took half the time it had taken by canal.

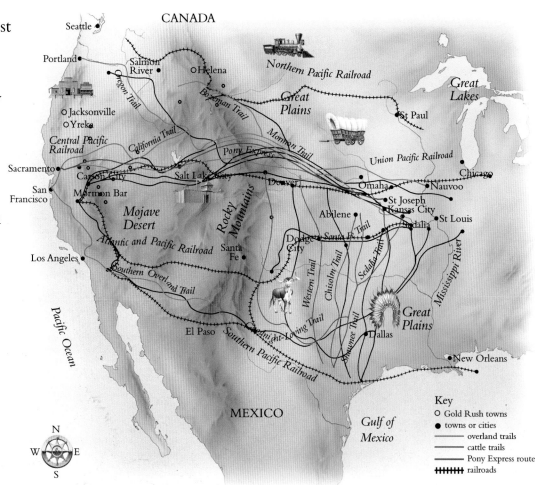

Key
○ Gold Rush towns
● towns or cities
—— overland trails
—— cattle trails
—— Pony Express route
╫╫╫╫ railroads

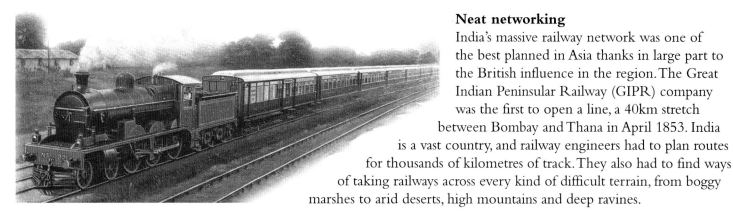

Neat networking

India's massive railway network was one of the best planned in Asia thanks in large part to the British influence in the region. The Great Indian Peninsular Railway (GIPR) company was the first to open a line, a 40km stretch between Bombay and Thana in April 1853. India is a vast country, and railway engineers had to plan routes for thousands of kilometres of track. They also had to find ways of taking railways across every kind of difficult terrain, from boggy marshes to arid deserts, high mountains and deep ravines.

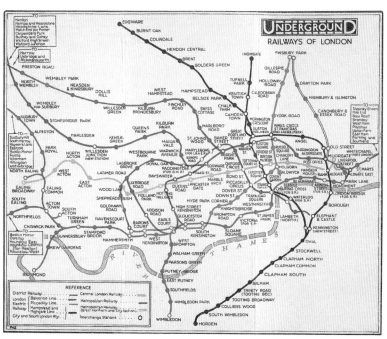

Designing ideas

Apart from the colour-coded routes, the 1927 map of the London Underground (at left) looks very different from the one of today (shown above). Early route maps were hard to follow because they tried to show the real geographical route of lines. More abstract, diagrammatical maps were the brainwave of British engineering draughtsman Henry C. Beck. His 1933 redesign of the London Underground map was inspired by electrical circuit diagrams. It makes no attempt to show the real geographical route and is not drawn to scale.

Surveying railway lines

Today computer programs are used to plan and design new railway routes. Data collected from on-the-ground surveying equipment (shown here), or the latest high-tech global positioning systems, is fed into a computer. The information is analyzed to ensure that the new rail route is feasible. The most direct route is not always the cheapest. Surveyors must consider factors such as difficult terrain, environmental benefits and existing rail networks when planning new routes.

BUILDING RAILWAYS

THERE WERE no automatic tools or building machines in the 1800s when the first railways were built. Everything was done by hand. Gangs of labourers called navvies moved mountains of earth using nothing but picks, shovels and barrows. Horses pulled the heaviest loads. Never before had so much earth been shifted, or so many bridges or tunnels built.

The challenge for the engineers who planned the railways was to construct tracks that were as level as possible. In the early days, locomotives had difficulty climbing even the slightest slope.

Channels called cuttings were dug or blasted through low hills, while mounds of earth and rock were piled into embankments to carry tracks over boggy or low ground. Railway routes had to avoid crossing high mountains and deep valleys. Sometimes, though, there was no getting around these obstacles. In the late 1800s, engineers such as Isambard Kingdom Brunel in Britain and Gustave Eiffel in France, began to design tunnels and bridges that were longer and stronger than the world had ever known.

Army on the march
Railways were carved out of the landscape during the 1800s by labourers called navigators or navvies. Originally, navvies built navigations, or canals, equipped with little more than picks and shovels. Gangs of navvies often moved from place to place, as one track, tunnel or bridge was completed and work on a new one started up. Some of the workers lived in temporary camps, while others rented rooms in nearby towns. Navvies had strong muscles, but many were also skilled carpenters, miners, stonemasons or blacksmiths.

The best route
Millions of tonnes of earth and rock were blasted away for cuttings and to make rail routes as level and as straight as possible. Even modern trains slow down on hills. Early steam locomotives just ground to a halt. Sharp curves would cause trains to derail. Alfred Nobel's development of dynamite in 1866 made blasting safer. It was more stable than earlier explosives.

FACT BOX
• At nearly 54km long, the Seikan Tunnel in Japan is presently the world's longest railway tunnel. The Alp Transit Link between Switzerland and Italy will beat this record by 3km. This tunnel is due to be completed in 2012.

• The world's longest double-decker road and railway suspension bridge is also in Japan. Called the Minami Bisan-seto Bridge, its main span is just over 1,100m long.

Bridging the valleys

There is not one perfect design for any bridge. In each case, a railway engineer has to take many factors into consideration before making the decision. These include the weight and frequency of traffic over the bridge, whether the underlying rock is hard or soft, the bridge's appearance in the landscape and the overall cost of the project.

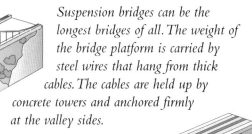

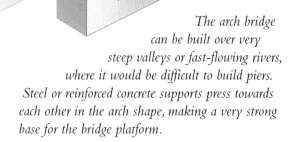

Suspension bridges can be the longest bridges of all. The weight of the bridge platform is carried by steel wires that hang from thick cables. The cables are held up by concrete towers and anchored firmly at the valley sides.

The beam bridge is made up of a horizontal platform supported on two or more piers (pillars). Sometimes a framework of steel girders is added. The girders act as a brace to strengthen and support the beam bridge between its piers.

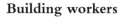

The arch bridge can be built over very steep valleys or fast-flowing rivers, where it would be difficult to build piers. Steel or reinforced concrete supports press towards each other in the arch shape, making a very strong base for the bridge platform.

Building workers

Thousands of skilled workers are involved in the manufacture of locomotives and rolling stock (passenger carriages and freight wagons). There are whole factories that specialize in making particular parts such as buffers or electric motors. At this factory, wheels and axles are being put together to be fitted to the bogie. Today, much of the work is carried out by machines, but some tasks, such as precision welding (joining of metal parts), still have to be done by hand.

Machines lighten the load

A Paved Concrete Track (PACT for short) machine is one way of taking the sweat out of laying railway track. It lays a trackbed of continuous concrete. Then, when the concrete is dry, other machines lift and clip the metal rails on top. In another automated method of track-laying, complete sections of track are made in factories with the rails already fixed to concrete sleepers. They are then transported to the site and lifted into position by cranes. Machines that could do such jobs automatically were introduced in the mid-1900s. They allowed the work to be done much more quickly, involving fewer people and a lot less effort.

LOAD-BEARING TUNNEL

TUNNELS OFTEN have to bear the weight of millions of tonnes of rocks and earth – or even water – above them. One way of preventing the tunnel collapsing is to make a continuous brick arch run along the length of the tunnel. Wedge-shaped keystones at the peak of the arch lock the whole structure together and support the arch and everything else above it. An arched roof is much stronger than a flat roof, because any weight above the tunnel is passed down through the sides of the arch and out towards the ground.

Between 1872 and 1882, a 15km-long railway tunnel was driven through Europe's highest mountains, the Alps, to link Switzerland to northern Italy. The St Gotthard tunnel was the greatest achievement in tunnel engineering of the time. Today, a long, train-like machine is used to build tunnels such as the Channel Tunnel. A big drill carves out the hole, sending the spoil backwards on a conveyor belt. Behind it, robotic cranes lift pre-cast concrete sections of the tunnel into place.

Keystone is key

Before a tunnel is built, engineers have to make sure the rock and soil are easy to cut through but firm enough not to collapse. A framework is used to build brick arches. The bricks are laid around both sides of the framework up towards the centre. When the central keystone is in place, the arch will support itself and the framework can be removed.

SUPPORTING ARCH

You will need: two wooden building blocks or house bricks, two pieces of thick card (width roughly the same as the length of the blocks or bricks), a few heavy pebbles.

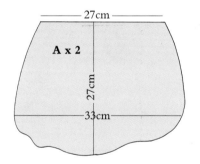

1 Place one of the pieces of card on top of the building blocks. Place pebbles on top as shown above. You will see that the tunnel roof sags under the weight.

2 Curve a second piece of card under the flat roof as shown. The roof supports the weight of the pebbles because the arch supports the flat section, making it stronger.

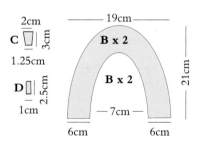

KEYSTONE

You will need: masking tape, piece of thick card measuring 46 x 27cm, two sheets of thick card measuring 36 x 30cm, ruler, pencil, scissors, piece of thin card measuring 44 x 40cm, newspaper, cup of flour, ½ cup of water, acrylic paints, paintbrush, water pot, piece of thin card (A4 size), glue and glue brush.

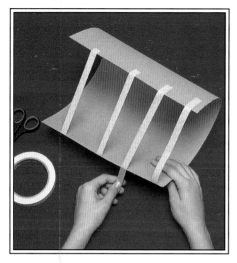

1 Tear off about four long strips of masking tape. Curve the 46 x 27cm rectangle of card lengthways. Use the tape to hold the curve in place as shown above.

2 Copy the two templates A on to two 36 x 30cm pieces of thick card. Cut out the shapes. Attach each one to the sides of the tunnel and secure with tape as shown above.

3 Fold the 44 x 40cm thin card in half. Copy the arch template B on to the card. Cut out to make two tunnel entrances. Stick these to the tunnel with masking tape as shown.

4 Scrunch newspaper into balls and tape to the tunnel and landscape. Mix the flour and water to make a thick paste. Dip newspaper strips in the paste. Layer them over the tunnel.

5 Leave to dry. When completely dry and hard, remove the tape and paint the tunnel and landscape green. Apply three coats, letting each one dry before you apply the next.

6 Paint the A4 size thin card to look like bricks. Draw and cut out templates C and D. Draw around C to make two keystones and D to make lots of bricks. Carefully cut the shapes out.

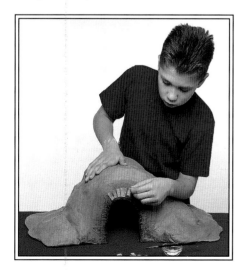

7 When the paint is dry, glue the keystones at the very top of each tunnel entrance. Then glue bricks around the arch either side of the keystone as shown. In a real tunnel, there would have been lots of central keystones running along the length of the tunnel.

8 Add finishing touches to your model using brown and green paints. Scrunch up newspaper into balls and dip them in the paste to make fake bushes. Leave them to dry and then paint them with brown and green paints. Do at least two or three coats. Leave them to dry between coats.

STATION STOP

ONCE PASSENGER trains began running in the 1830s, people needed special buildings where they could buy tickets and shelter from the weather while they waited to board. No one had ever designed or built railway stations before. The owners of the new railway companies wanted to make as much money as possible, so they had big, impressive mainline stations built to attract customers. Long platforms were essential for trains with many carriages, so that passengers could get on and off trains safely. There also had to be waiting rooms and restaurants, as well as offices where station staff worked.

London's Euston Station was the first to have separate platforms for arrivals and departures. This station was also among the earliest to have a metal and glass roof over the platforms. Euston was opened in 1838. From then on, most big stations had glass and metal roofs. They were relatively cheap and easy to build, and they also let in a lot of daylight, which helped to save money on artificial lighting. In those days, lighting was provided by expensive gas lamps.

Housed in style

An early steam train puffs out of the first circular engine shed, built in 1847 in London. Even the engine sheds where steam locomotives were housed for maintenance or repair were well designed. In the middle of these circular sheds was a turntable with short sections of track arranged around it, rather like the spokes of a wheel. Locomotives were parked on each section of track and released when they were needed for a journey.

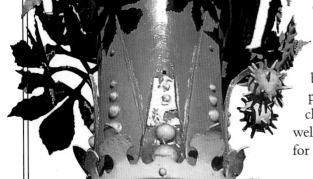

Decorative ironwork

The iron pillars of stations in the 1900s were cast into a fantastic variety of shapes and then beautifully painted. At this time, cast iron was one of the latest building materials. Cast-iron pillars and arches were fairly cheap and quick to erect, as well as being a strong framework for station walls and roofs.

Temples of fashion

Bristol Temple Meads Station, Britain, looked like this in the 1800s. Engineers and architects tried to make their stations look stylish as well as be functional. During the 1800s, it was fashionable to copy the great building styles of the past. Bristol Temple Meads Station imitated the magnificent Gothic cathedrals and churches of medieval times. Small country stations, on the other hand, often looked like cottages or suburban villas.

Classical station

The main station building of Washington Union Station in the USA is typical of stations built in the early 1900s. It has a lofty vaulted ceiling and interiors made of panelled wood. It was opened in 1907 and was built by the Washington Terminal Company, which was specially formed by railways serving the city.

German hub

Busy Cologne *Hauptbahnhof* (main station) is at the centre of Germany's vast rail network in the north-west of the country. The old steel-and-glass train shed was damaged during World War II (1939–45) but was later rebuilt. The front of the station has today been completely rebuilt with a more modern frontage.

Simple fare

Unlike the grand stations that serve cities, country stations are often very basic, such as this one at Pargothan, India. There are no platforms, and passengers climb into the trains from the track.

Single span

Atocha is the terminus of Spain's *Alta Velocita Española* (AVE) high-speed rail link between the capital, Madrid, and Seville in southern Spain. It was built in the early 1890s, and it serves all routes to the south, east and south-east of Madrid. It is Spain's largest station and is famous for its single-span arched roof.

FACT BOX
• The world's largest railway station is Beijing West Railway Station in China. It covers 54 hectares and is bigger than the world's smallest country, the Vatican City in Rome, Italy.

• The world's highest railway station is at Condor in Bolivia, South America. It is at 4,786m above sea level, 308m higher than the Matterhorn Mountain in the Alps.

• The world's busiest railway station is Clapham Junction in south London, Britain. More than 2,000 trains pass through the station every 24 hours.

SHRINKING WORLD

Ticket to ride
Cheap, speedy trains meant that for the first time ordinary people, rather than only the wealthy, could travel for pleasure. Train companies began offering day-excursion trips in the early 1830s. Outings to the seaside were particularly popular.

Ceremonial spike
On 10 May 1869, a golden spike was hammered into the track when the world's first transcontinental railway was completed, linking the east and west coasts of the USA. The railway was built by two companies, and the spike marked the meeting place of the two tracks at Promontory Summit in Utah.

BEFORE THE coming of the railways, the fastest way to travel was on horseback. Even though the swiftest racehorse can gallop at more than 60km/h, it cannot keep this speed up for longer than a few minutes. Trains, on the other hand, can travel at high speed for hours on end. They can also transport hundreds of people at a time, or tens of wagon-loads of freight, across vast distances. As more and more railway lines began snaking across the countryside, life speeded up and the world seemed to grow smaller. People and goods could reach places they had never been to before.

During the 1800s, railway technology spread from Britain all over the world. Tracks were laid between towns and cities at first. Later, railways slowly grew to link countries and span continents. The world's first transcontinental railway was completed in the USA in 1869. The expansion of the railway system in the USA was rapid. Railways were built through areas that had not yet been settled and played an important part in opening up many parts of the country.

FACT BOX
• With around 240,000km of rail track, the USA has the world's longest network of railways – just about enough to wrap around the Equator six times.

• It takes just over eight days to ride the entire length of the world's longest railway, the Trans-Siberian line in Asia. This railway, which opened in 1903, runs for 9,611km from Moscow to Vladivostok.

Desert runner
When surveyors planned the western section of Australia's transcontinental railway, they plotted what is still today the world's longest stretch of straight track. This 478km section lies within a vast, treeless desert called the Nullarbor Plain between Port Augusta and Kalgoorlie in southwestern Australia. The western section of this transcontinental railway opened in 1917. The luxury Indian Pacific service was launched in 1969. Today, the 3,961km journey from Sydney to Perth takes just under three days.

Ruling by rail

A steam train passes over a bridge in India. During the 1800s, the British gradually introduced railway networks to India and other countries in the British Empire. By speeding up the movement of government officials and the military, trains helped Britain keep control of its empire. Trade goods could be moved more quickly, too, which benefited British-owned companies. By 1939, India had more than 50,000km of track.

Keeping up with the times

The time in any place in the world is calculated from Greenwich Mean Time, which is the local time at 0 degrees longitude at Greenwich in London, England. Local time in other countries is calculated as either behind or in front of Greenwich Mean Time. Before the railways, even cities within the same country kept their own local time, and accurate timetables were impossible. Time-keeping had to be standardized if people were to know when to catch their trains. British railway companies standardized time-keeping using Greenwich Mean Time in 1847.

Coast-to-coast challenge

Pulled by diesel locomotives, passenger trains can today make the spectacular 4,650-km journey across Canada in three days. When the Canadian Pacific transcontinental railway was completed in 1887, the trip took steam trains about a week. The biggest challenge for the army of workers who built the railway was taking the track through the Rocky Mountains – at Kicking Horse Pass, it climbs to 1,624m.

A PASSION FOR TRAINS

In 1830, a young British actress called Fanny Kemble wrote to a friend about her railway journey pulled by a "brave little she-dragon … the magical machine with its wonderful flying white breath and rhythmical unvarying pace".

Over the years, all sorts of people – young and old, male and female, rich and poor – have caught Fanny's enthusiasm for trains. Some people love travelling on them, enjoying the scenery flickering past the windows and chatting to the strangers they meet on the journey. Others are happiest when they are standing at the end of a platform, spotting trains and noting down locomotive numbers. Other enthusiasts spend their spare time building their own private museum of railway history. They collect anything from old railway tickets, timetables and luggage labels, to early signalling equipment, station clocks and locomotive numberplates. Some people 'collect' journeys and take pride in travelling on some of the world's most famous railways.

Reliving the past

You can still ride a real steam train today, although in most countries only where short stretches of line have been preserved. Many classic locomotives of the past are on display in railway museums. Visitors can usually get close enough to touch, and sometimes they are allowed to climb up inside the driver's cab. You should never get this close when spotting working trains, however. Always stand well back on the platform, and never climb down on to the track.

Railway mania

The walls of this railway enthusiast's room are decorated with prizes collected during years of hunting through junk shops and car-boot sales, and attending auctions. Lamps and many other pieces of railway and station equipment came on to the market in Britain during the 1960s, when the government closed down hundreds of country railway stations and branch lines.

Collecting signals

During the late 1900s, many old semaphore signals like these were made redundant. They were replaced with colour-light signals controlled from power signal boxes. Much of the old signalling was purchased by Britain's heritage railways, but a few railway enthusiasts bought signals for their gardens. The ones in this picture are Great Western Railway design signals, dating from the 1940s.

Museum pieces

The Baltimore and Ohio Museum was set up in the city of Baltimore, USA, by the Baltimore and Ohio Railroad in 1953. The main exhibits are displayed in a full-circle roundhouse in what used to be the railway's workshops. The exhibits feature a full range of locomotives from the last 180 years. They include a replica of the first US steam locomotive of 1829 and a recently retired diesel passenger locomotive.

Tickets, please

Railway tickets and timetables are all collectable items for those who are interested in trains and train journeys.
A trainspotter's handbook and a set of railway timetables are essential equipment for the serious train enthusiast. You can buy handbooks at specialist bookshops. They list all the working locomotives in a particular country.

WARNING BOX

• Never go trainspotting without first asking the permission of your parents and telling them where you are going.
• At stations, always stand well back from the platform edge.
• Railway lines have fences on either side to keep people a safe distance from the track. Stand behind the fence – never climb over it.
• Modern trains are fast and make very little noise. If you disregard these simple rules, you will be risking your life.

Number crunching

Locomotives have numberplates in much the same way that cars do. The plate is usually on the front of the engine. Unlike a car numberplate, however, some train numberplates have no letters in them. Trainspotters aim to collect the number of every working locomotive, but with so many locomotives in operation, it is a very time-consuming hobby.

TRAINS IN MINIATURE

MODEL TRAINS are just about as old as steam locomotives. The first ones were not for children, though. They were made for the locomotive manufacturers of the early 1800s to show how the newly invented, full-sized machines worked.

Although most toy trains are miniature versions of the real thing, they come in different scales or sizes. Most are built in O scale, which is $\frac{1}{48}$th the size of the real train. The smallest are Z scale, which is $\frac{1}{220}$th the size of a real train. Z-scale locomotives are small enough to fit inside a matchbox! It is extremely difficult to make accurate models to this small a scale, so Z-scale train sets are usually the hardest to find in shops and the most expensive to buy.

All the exterior working parts of the original are shown on the best model locomotives, from the chimney on top of the engine to the coupling and connecting rods.

Smile, please
In the early 1900s, a few lucky children owned their own toy train. Some early toy trains had clockwork motors or tiny steam engines. Others were 'carpet-runners'. These were simply pushed or pulled along the floor.

Top-class toys
One British manufacturer of model trains was Bassett-Lowke, the maker of this fine model of *Princess Elizabeth*. Another manufacturer was Hornby, whose trains first went on sale in the 1920s. Hornby quickly grew into Britain's most popular model. Many different real-life models were produced. There were freight wagons and tankers, as well as passenger coaches with opening doors.

A model world
In the 1920s, toymakers began producing small-scale table-top model railways. Stations and track took up less space than older, larger-scale models had needed. Many of these models were electric-powered and made from cast metal and tinplate by the German firm Bing. Today, these models are very valuable.

The German connection

Model trains are being made at the Fleischmann Train Factory, Nuremberg, Germany. Fleischmann produces highly detailed models of the full range of modern European trains. Like earlier model-railway manufacturers, Fleischmann does not only make the trains. Collectors and model-railway enthusiasts can also buy everything that goes to make up a railway, including signals and signal boxes, lights and level crossings, engine sheds, bridges and tunnels. There are even stations and platforms with miniature newspaper kiosks, station staff and passengers.

Model behaviour

In the earliest train sets, miniature locomotives hauled wagons and carriages on a never-ending journey around a circular track. Gradually, toymakers began selling more complex layouts, with several sets of track linked by points. Trains could switch from one track to another, just as in real railways.

Ticket to ride

Model trains come in all sizes, including those that are large enough for children and adults to ride on. These miniature trains have all the working parts and features of their full-sized parents, including a tiny firebox which the driver stokes with coal to keep the train chuffing along.

In the USA in the late 1890s, small-gauge lines were appearing at showgrounds and in amusement parks. By the 1920s, longer miniature railways were being built in Britain and Germany. Today, many theme parks feature a miniature railway.

MODEL LOCOMOTIVES

A precision toy

As manufacturing techniques improved, so toy trains became increasingly sophisticated. Today, accurate, working, scale models have all the features of full-size working trains.

TOY TRAINS started to go on sale during the mid–1800s. Early toy trains were made of brightly painted wood, and often had a wooden track to run along. Soon, metal trains went on sale, many of them made from tinplate (thin sheets of iron or steel coated with tin). Some of these metal toy trains had wind-up clockwork motors. Clockwork toy trains were first sold in the USA during the 1880s. The most sophisticated model trains were steam-powered, with tiny engines fired by methylated-spirit burners. Later model trains were powered by electric motors.

Railway companies often devised special colour schemes, called liveries, for their locomotives and carriages. Steam locomotives had brass and copper decoration, and some also carried the company's special logo or badge. Many toy trains are also painted in the livery of a real railway company. The shape of the locomotive you can make in this project has a cab typical of the real locomotives made in the 1910s.

TOY TRAIN

You will need: *26 x 26cm card, masking tape, scissors, ruler, pencil, 10 x 10cm card, glue and glue brush, card for templates, paints, paintbrush, water pot, underframe from earlier project, two drawing pins, 11 x 1cm red card, split pin.*

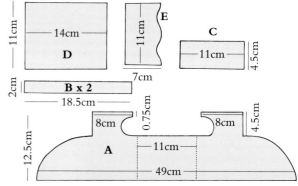

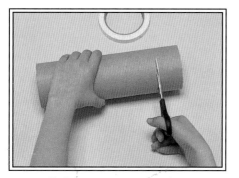

1 Roll the 26 x 26cm card into an 8-cm diameter tube. Secure it with masking tape. Cut a 6-cm slit, 5cm from one end of the tube.

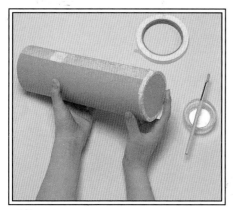

2 Hold the tube upright on the 10 x 10cm piece of card. Draw around it. Cut this circle out. Glue the circle to the tube end farthest away from the slit. Tape to secure.

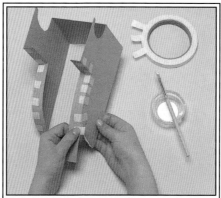

3 Copy and cut out templates. Fold template A along the dotted lines. Fold templates B across, 4.5cm from one end. Glue both strips to the cab as shown and secure with tape.

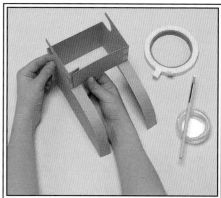

4 When the glue is dry, gently peel off the masking tape. Now glue on template C as shown above. Hold it in place with masking tape until the glue dries.

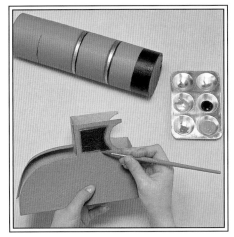

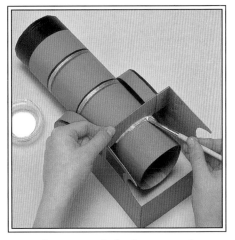

5 Apply two coats of green paint to the outside of the locomotive. Let the first coat dry before applying the second. Then paint the black parts. Add the red and gold last.

6 Glue around the bottom edge of the cab front C. Put a little glue over the slit in the tube. Fit the front of the cab into the slit. Leave the locomotive to one side to dry.

7 Give roof template D two coats of black paint. Let the paint dry between coats. Glue the top edges of the cab, and place the black roof on top. Leave until dry and firm.

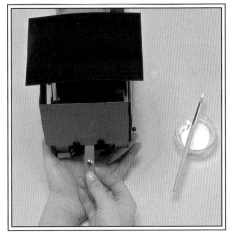

8 Glue the bottom of the cylindrical part of the train to the underframe you made in the *Underframe* project. Press drawing pins into back of cab and underframe.

9 Glue both sides of one end of the red strip. Slot this between the underframe and the cab, between the drawing pins. When firm, fold the strip and insert the split pin.

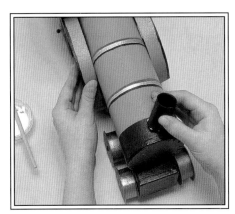

10 Paint one side of template E black. When dry, roll into a tube and secure with masking tape. Glue wavy edge and secure to front of locomotive as shown above.

Just like a real locomotive, the basic colour of your model train has been enhanced with red, black and gold decoration. The locomotive is now ready to run on the railway line you made in the Making Tracks *project. The driver and fireman would have shared the cab of the locomotive. The driver controlled the speed of the train, following the signals and track speed restrictions. The fireman ensured a good supply of steam by stoking the fire and filling the boiler with water.*

SIGNALS AND SIGNALLING

THE EARLIEST railways were single tracks that ran directly between one place and another. Later, more tracks were laid and branched off these main lines. Trains were able to cross from one line to another on movable sections of track called points.

To avoid crashes, a system of signals was needed to show drivers if the track ahead was clear. The first signallers stood beside the track and waved flags during daylight or lamps at night. From 1841, human signallers were replaced by signals called semaphores on posts with wooden arms.

By 1889, three basics of rail safety were established by law in Britain – block, brake and lock. Block involved stopping one train until the one in front had passed by. Brakes are an obvious safety feature on passenger trains. Lock meant that points and signals had to be interlocked, so that a lever in the signal box could not be pulled without changing both the point and the signal.

Hand signals
The first people to be responsible for train safety in Britain were the railway police. The policemen used flags and lamps to direct the movements of trains. In the absence of flags, signals were given by hand. One arm outstretched horizontally meant 'line clear', one arm raised meant 'caution' and both arms raised meant 'danger, stop'.

Mechanical signals
A railway policeman operates a Great Western Railway disc and crossbar signal. The disc and crossbar were at right angles and rotated so the driver could either see the full face of the disc, meaning 'go', or the crossbar, meaning 'stop'.

Lighting up the night
Electric signals were not used until the 1920s, when colour-light signals were introduced. Colour-light signals look like road traffic lights. A green light means the track is clear, red shows danger and yellow means caution. Colour-light signals, such as these in France, are accompanied by displays showing the number of the signal, speed restrictions and other information for train drivers.

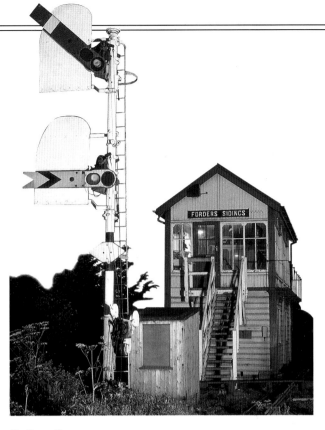

Signal improvements

This hand-operated signal frame features details dating from the 1850s, when a signalling system called interlocking was introduced. Signals and points were interlocked (linked) so that a single lever moved a signal and the set of points it protected at the same time. Signal box levers were moved by hand to set signals and points in those days. In many countries today, signals are set automatically by computers that are housed in a central signalling control room.

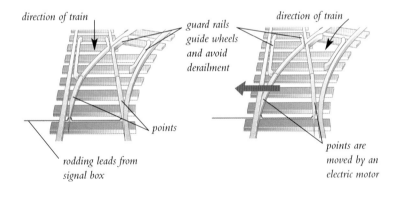

direction of train

guard rails guide wheels and avoid derailment

direction of train

points

rodding leads from signal box

points are moved by an electric motor

Safety first

Semaphore signals such as these made a major difference to railway safety when they were introduced during the 1840s. At first, railway companies throughout the world used semaphore signals with oil lamps behind coloured glass to show if the track was clear at night (green light) or at danger (red light). From the 1920s, many countries upgraded their systems by introducing electric colour-light signals.

Points and humpyard

Trains are switched from one track to another using points. Part of the track, called the blade, moves so that the wheels are guided smoothly from one route on to the other. The blade moves as a result of a signaller pulling a lever in the signal box. The blade and lever are connected by a system of metal rods, and the lever cannot be pulled unless the signal is clear. From the late 1800s, railway companies built humpyards. These made it easier to shunt freight wagons together to make a freight train. As the wagons went over a hump in the yard, they uncoupled. When they went down the hump, they could be switched into different sidings using a set of points.

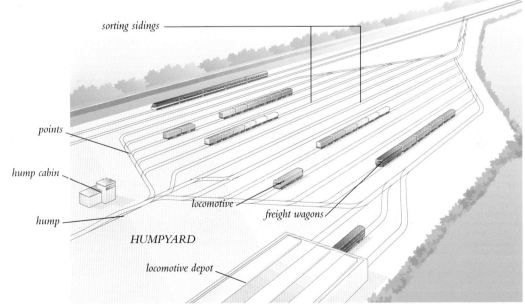

sorting sidings

points

hump cabin

hump

HUMPYARD

locomotive

freight wagons

locomotive depot

SAFETY FIRST

ACCIDENTS ARE a tragic feature of railway travel today, but trains remain the safest form of land transport in most countries. Modern technology is largely responsible for the improvements in rail safety. In Britain, trains are fitted with an Automatic Warning System (AWS). If the signal indicates that the track ahead is clear, electric magnets between the rails send a message to equipment under the train. This causes a bell to sound in the driver's cab. If the signal is not clear, the magnet stays 'dead', and a horn sounds in the cab. If the driver does not react, the brakes come on automatically. An improved system, called Train Protection and Warning System (TPWS), uses existing AWS but also provides an automatic stop at a red signal and a speed trap in advance of the signal.

A more advanced system is Automatic Train Protection (ATP). The train picks up electronic messages from the track, and they tell the driver to slow down or stop the train. If he or she fails to respond, there is a warning and the brakes come on. ATP also slows or stops the train if it exceeds the speed limit.

On collision course

Head-on crashes were more common in the early days of the railways, even though there were far fewer trains. On some routes, there was only a single-track line. A train heading towards a station was in danger of meeting another train leaving it. In most countries today, trains are timetabled so that no two are on the same line at the same time. This situation can only arise if a train passes a stop signal at a set of points.

Japanese crash

A crane lifts a derailed train along the Hanshin Railway near Shinzaike Station. The accident was caused by an earthquake that devastated the city of Kobe on the Japanese island of Honshu in 1995. Several stations and several kilometres of elevated railway lines were destroyed on the three main lines that run from Kobe to Osaka.

Control centre

From the 1960s, signalling over large areas has been controlled from centralized signal boxes. The signal boxes have a control panel that displays all the routes, signals and points that the signal box controls. Signallers set up safe routes for trains in the area by operating switches and buttons. Signals work automatically, and the points change using electronic controls. This ensures trains cannot get on routes where there is an oncoming train. In the most modern signalling centres, the routes appear on computer screens. The signaller uses a cursor to set up routes instead of using buttons and switches.

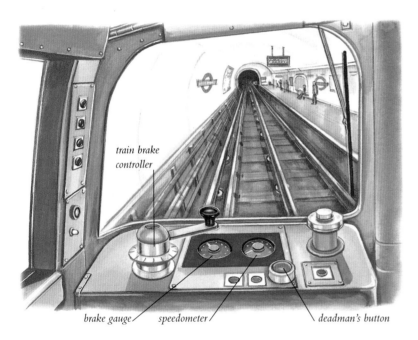

train brake controller

brake gauge   speedometer   deadman's button

In the driving seat

The control desk of a London Underground, or 'Tube', train has a number of standard safety features. The train brake controller is a manual control to slow the train. The deadman's button must be pressed down continually by the driver while the train is moving. If the driver collapses, the button comes up and the train stops.

Onboard safety

In the event of an emergency, passengers will always find standard safety devices, such as fire extinguishers and first-aid kits, on board a train.

Buffer zone

Buffers stop trains at the end of a line. They are made of metal or wood and metal and are fixed to the track. They are strong enough to absorb much of the energy of a colliding train. Signals control a train's speed so that even if a train collides with the bufferstops, it is usually travelling slowly.

Coupling up

A locomotive is joined up to a wagon by a connection called a coupling. At first, chains or rigid bars were used to join carriages. Later, a rigid hook at the end of one vehicle connected to chains on the front of the next. From the late 1800s, couplings made from steel castings and springs were used, but uncoupling was done by hand. Today, passenger trains couple and uncouple automatically.

BRAKE VAN

FEW EARLY steam locomotives had brakes. If the driver needed to stop quickly, he had to throw the engine into reverse. By the early 1860s, braking systems for steam locomotives had been invented. Some passenger carriages also had their own handbrakes that were operated by the carriage guards. A brake van was added to the back of trains, too, but its brakes were operated by a guard riding inside.

The problem was that the train driver had no control over the rest of the train. When he wanted to stop, he had to blow the engine whistle to warn each of the guards to apply their brakes. The brakes on a locomotive and its carriages or wagons needed to be linked. This was made possible by the invention of an air-braking system in 1869. When the driver applies the brakes, compressed air travels along pipes linking all parts of the train and presses brake shoes. Air brakes are now used on nearly all the world's railways.

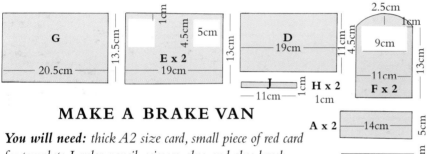

MAKE A BRAKE VAN

You will need: *thick A2 size card, small piece of red card for template J, ruler, pencil, scissors, glue and glue brush, masking tape, acrylic paints, paintbrush, water pot, two 3-cm lengths of 0.5-cm diameter dowel, pair of compasses.*

1 Copy the templates on to card and cut them out. Glue templates A, B and C together to make the underframe as shown. Tape over the joins to secure them.

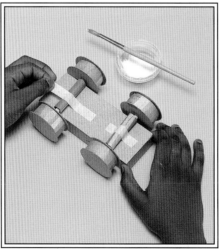

2 Make and paint two pairs of small wheels (diameter 5cm) following steps 1 to 5 in the *Underframe* project. Glue and tape the wheel pairs to the underframe.

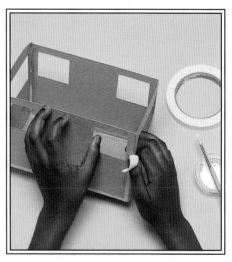

3 Glue the bottom edges of the van sides (E) to the van base (D). Then glue on the van ends (F). Secure the joins with masking tape until the glue is dry.

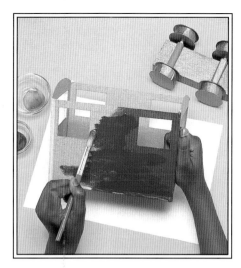

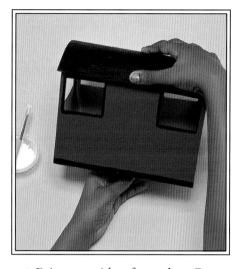

4 Paint the brake van brown with black details and the wheels and underframe black and silver. Apply two coats of paint, letting each one dry between coats.

5 Paint one side of template G black. Let the paint dry before applying a second coat. Glue the top edges of the van. Bend the roof to fit on the top of the van as shown.

6 Apply glue to the top surface of the underframe. Stick the brake van centrally on top. Press together until the glue holds firm. Leave to dry completely.

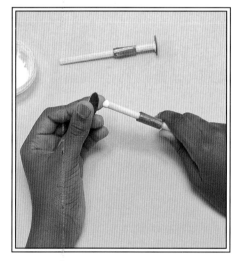

7 Roll up templates I into two 2-cm tubes to fit loosely over the dowel. Tape to hold and paint them silver. Paint the buffer templates H black and stick on each dowel.

8 Use compasses to pierce two holes 2.5cm from each side of the van and 1.5cm up. Enlarge with a pencil. Glue the end of each dowel buffer. Slot it into the hole. Leave to dry.

9 Cut a slot between the buffers. Fold red card template J in half. Glue each end to form a loop. Push the closed end into the slot. Hold it in place until the glue dries.

The brake van will also run on the tracks you made in the Making Tracks *project. You can also join the red-card coupling to join the brake van to the model locomotive you made in the* Toy Train *project. On old-style railways, the brake van was at the back of the train so that the guard could make sure that all the carriages stayed coupled. The brake van had one of two brake systems. One had hand-operated brakes that worked on the tread of the brake van's wheels. The other had a valve that allowed the guard to apply air brakes to all vehicles in the train.*

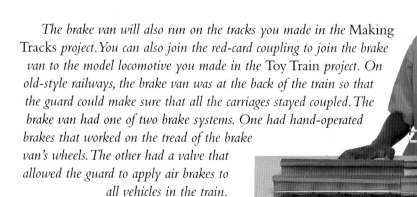

HAULING FREIGHT

M OST OF the traffic on the world's railways is made up of freight trains that transport goods such as coal and iron ore from mines and cloth and other manufactured goods from factories. The earliest freight trains were slow because they did not have effective braking systems. Technical developments now mean that freight trains can run much faster than before.

Freight trains made a vast difference to everyday life as the rail networks expanded and brought the country nearer to the city. For the first time, fresh food could be delivered quickly from country farms to city markets. People could also afford to heat their homes. The price of coal for household fires came down because moving coal by train was cheaper and faster than by horse-drawn carts or canal.

In the mid-1900s, motor vehicles and aircraft offered an alternative way of transporting freight. However, concerns about congestion and the environment mean that freight trains continue to be the cheapest, quickest and most environmentally friendly way of hauling a large volume of freight overland.

Four-legged freight service
The world's first public railway opened in 1803 – for horse-drawn freight wagons. The Surrey Iron Railway ran for a little more than 13km between Wandsworth and Croydon near London. It went past a number of mills and factories. The factory owners paid a toll to use the railway and supplied their own horses and wagons.

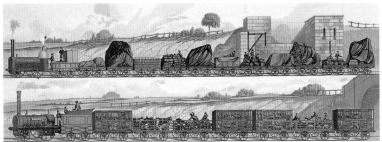

Rolling stock
Freight wagons were ramshackle affairs when the first steam trains began running during the 1820s and 1830s. They had metal wheels but, unlike locomotives, they were mainly built from wood. Their design was based on the horse-drawn carts or coal wagons they were replacing. Waterproof tarpaulins were tied over goods to protect them from the weather.

Slow but steady
In the early 1800s, the first steam locomotives hauled coal wagons called chaldrons from collieries to ships on nearby rivers. The locomotives were not very powerful. They could pull only a few wagons at a time. Going any faster would have been dangerous because neither the locomotives nor the wagons had much in the way of brakes!

Mail by rail

Post was first carried by the world's railways in the 1830s. A special mail carriage was introduced in Britain in 1838. Post Office workers on board sorted the mail for delivery while the train was moving. Modern versions of these travelling post offices still operate today.

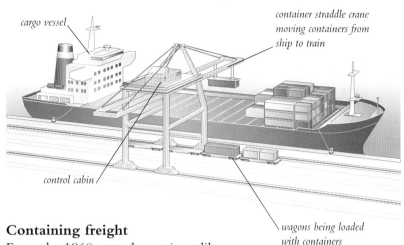

cargo vessel

container straddle crane moving containers from ship to train

control cabin

wagons being loaded with containers

Containing freight

From the 1960s, metal containers like giant boxes have transported goods by sea, rail and road. They are a way of combining different methods of transporting goods in the most effective way possible. The containers are simply lifted from one vehicle to another using large cranes called straddle cranes. The trains usually have specially designed flat wagons on to which the containers are locked into position. The containers remain sealed, apart from when they are inspected by customs officials.

Bulk transportation

Today, freight trains mainly transport heavy, bulky loads such as coal, iron ore, grain or building materials. Smaller, lighter goods are usually sent by road or air. Railway companies pioneered the idea of specially designed vehicles for different types of freight – tankers for liquids such as milk or chemicals, for example, and hoppers that tip sideways for unloading gravel or coal.

FACT BOX
- Today, freight trains haul bulky loads, such as coal, oil and minerals, in purpose-built wagons.

- As many as 10,000 freight trains criss-cross the USA every day.

- Some of the world's freight trains have 200 wagons and can be up to 4km long.

- Modern diesel and electric freight trains can haul heavy loads at speeds of up to 120km/h.

Chinese circle

From the mid-1900s, Chinese electric locomotives such as this hauled ore hoppers. The trains carried iron ore to be smelted in blast furnaces on an 80-km circular line. The locomotives were based on a Swiss design. They had a sloping front so that the driver could see easily from the cab.

GOING UNDERGROUND

RAILWAY NETWORKS made it easier for people to travel from the country to cities and towns to shop or work. During the 1800s, the streets within cities became extremely crowded with people and traffic. One way of coping with the problem of moving around the cities was to tunnel underground.

The world's first underground passenger railway opened in 1863. It was the Metropolitan Line between Paddington Station and Farringdon Street in London, Britain. Steam locomotives hauled the passenger carriages, and smoke in the tunnels was a big problem. The locomotives were fitted with structures called condensers that were supposed to absorb the smoke, but they did not work properly. Passengers on the trains travelled through a fog-like darkness. Those waiting at the stations choked on the smoke drifting out from the tunnels.

The answer was to use electric trains, and the first underground electric railway opened in London in 1890. Today, nearly every major city in the world has its own underground railway system.

Cut-and-cover construction
The first underground passenger railways were built using a new method called cut-and-cover construction. A large trench – usually 10m wide by 5m deep – was cut into the earth along the railway's proposed route. Then the trench was lined with brickwork and it was roofed over. After that, the streets were re-laid on top of the tunnel.

Tunnel maze
This cross-section of the underground system in central London in 1864 shows the proposed route of the new Charing Cross line beneath the existing Metropolitan Line. Deep-level underground railways were not built until 1890, when developments such as ways of digging deeper tunnels, electric locomotives, better lifts and escalators became a reality.

Underground shelters
Londoners came up with another use for their city's warren of underground railway tunnels during World War II (1939–45). They used them as deep shelters from night-time bombing raids. The electric lines were switched off, and people slept wherever they could find enough room to lie down. Canteens were set up on many platforms. More than half a million litres of tea and cocoa were served every night.

Keeping up with the times

The Washington DC Metro was opened in 1976 in the USA. It is one of the world's newest and most up-to-date underground railways. The trains have no drivers and the entire network is controlled automatically by a computerized central control system. Passengers travelling in the air-conditioned carriages have a smooth, fast ride due to the latest techniques in train and track construction. The airy, 183m-long stations are much more spacious than those built in the early 1900s.

FACT BOX

• The world's busiest underground system is the New York City subway with 468 stations. The first section opened in 1904.

• The London Underground is the world's longest system. It has more than 400km of route.

• The world's second electric underground railway was the 4km-long line in Budapest, Hungary. It opened in 1896.

Overground undergrounds

Work started on the first 10km-long section of the Paris *Metro* in 1898 and took over two years to complete. The engineers who designed early underground railway systems, such as the Paris *Metro*, often found it quicker and easier to take sections above ground, particularly when crossing rivers. The station entrances were designed by French architect Hector Guimard in the then-fashionable Art Nouveau style. They made the Paris *Metro* one of the most distinctive and stylish underground systems in the world.

Mechanical earthworm

The cutting head of a Tunnel-Boring Machine (TBM), which was used to bore the Channel Tunnel between England and France. The 8m-wide cutting head is covered with diamond-studded teeth. As the TBM rotates, the teeth rip through the earth. The waste material, or spoil, falls on to a conveyor belt and is transported to the surface. The cutting head grips against the sides of the tunnel and inches farther forward under the pressure of huge rams. As the tunnel is cut, cranes line the tunnel with curved concrete segments that arrive on conveyors at the top and bottom of the TBM.

RIDING HIGH

IN SOME of the world's cities, the solution to overcrowded streets was to build railway networks above ground level. The earliest kind of overhead trains ran on a twin-rail track. The track was raised above the ground on arching, viaduct-like supports. These 'elevated railways' were built in several American and European cities from the mid-1800s onward.

Today, some overhead trains run along a single rail called a monorail. Some are suspended systems in which the train hangs beneath the rail. Others are straddle systems in which the train sits over the rail.

Twin-rail systems called Light Rapid Transit (LRT) are now more common than monorails. They are described as 'light' because they carry fewer people and therefore need lighter-weight vehicles and track than mainline, or 'heavy', railways. In many cities, LRT railcars are like a cross between a tram and a train. They run on rails through town and city streets, as well as through underground tunnels and along elevated tracks.

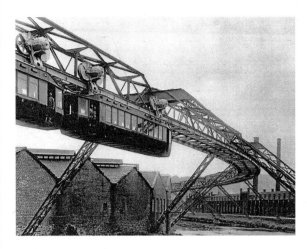

Wonder of Wuppertal
The oldest working monorail in the world is located in Wuppertal, Germany. Almost 20 million passengers have travelled along the 13.3km-long route since it opened in 1901. It is suspended about 10m above the ground. The wheels run along the top of the rail.

Flying train
Inventor George Bennie's experimental monorail was one of the strangest ever built. The streamlined machine was named the Railplane. It had aeroplane propellers front and back to thrust it along. It first 'flew' in July 1930, along a 40m-long test line over a railway track near Glasgow, Scotland.

Climb every mountain
The Paris funicular railway climbs to the city's highest point, the top of Montmartre. Funicular railways were invented during the 1800s and are used to move carriages up and down hillsides or steep slopes. Usually, there are two parallel tracks. Each one has a passenger-carrying car attached. In the early days, each car carried a large water tank that was filled with water at the top of the slope and emptied at the bottom. The extra weight of the car going down pulled the lighter car up. Later funicular railways have winding drums powered by electricity to haul a cable up and down.

Tomorrow's world

During the 1950s, American film producer Walt Disney wanted to have a monorail for his futuristic Tomorrowland attraction when he built his first Disneyland theme park in California. The monorail opened in 1959 and was an immediate success with visitors. Disney was trying to promote monorails as the transport system of the future, but his railway had just the opposite effect. For many years, monorails were seen as little more than amusement-park rides.

Not everyone's darling

The monorail system in Sydney, Australia, links the heart of the city to a tourist development in nearby Darling Harbour. It has proved to be popular since it opened in 1988, carrying about 30,000 people a day along its 3.5km-long route. Many people who lived in Sydney were concerned that the elevated route would be an eyesore, particularly in older parts of the city. Protesters tried hard to block the monorail's construction. Today, it has become part of everyday life for many people who live in Sydney.

London's LRT

The Docklands Light Railway in London opened in 1987. It was Britain's first Light Rapid Transit (LRT) to have driverless vehicles controlled by a computerized control system. However, it was not Britain's first LRT. That prize went to Newcastle's Tyne and Wear Metro, which began running in 1980. LRTs provide a frequent service, with unstaffed stations and automatic ticket machines. Many cities throughout the world have chosen to install them in preference to monorails because they are cheaper to run.

MONORAIL

MONORAILS DATE back to the 1820s. As with early trains, these early monorails were pulled by horses and carried heavy materials such as building bricks, rather than passengers. About 60 years later, engineers designed steam locomotives that hauled carriages along A-shaped frameworks. However, neither the trains nor the carriages were very stable. Loads had to be carefully balanced on either side of the A-frame to stop them tipping off.

Today's monorails are completely stable, with several sets of rubber wheels to give a smooth ride. They are powered by electricity, and many are driverless. Like fully automatic LRTs, driverless monorail trains are controlled by computers that tell them when to stop, start, speed up or slow down.

Monorails are not widely used today because they are more expensive to run than two-track railways. The special monorail track costs more to build and is more of an eyesore than two-track lines. The cars cannot be switched from one track to another, and it is expensive to change or extend a monorail line.

Staying on track
Vertical sets of running wheels carry the weight of this modern monorail and keep it on top of the huge rail. Other horizontal sets of wheels, called guides and stabilizers, run along the sides of the rail. They keep the train on course and stop it from tipping when it goes around bends.

MODEL MONORAIL

You will need: sheet of protective paper, 72cm length of wood (4cm wide and 4cm deep), acrylic paints, paintbrush, water pot, 67cm length of plastic curtain rail (with screws, end fittings and four plastic runners), saw, screwdriver, sheet of red card, pencil, ruler, scissors, double-sided sticky tape, 18cm length of 2.5cm thick foam board, glue and glue brush, black felt tip pen.

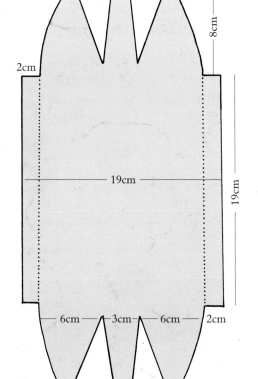

2cm · 8cm · 19cm · 19cm · 6cm · 3cm · 6cm · 2cm · 1.5cm

1 Cover the work surface with paper to protect it. Then paint the block of wood yellow. Let the first coat dry thoroughly before applying a second coat of paint.

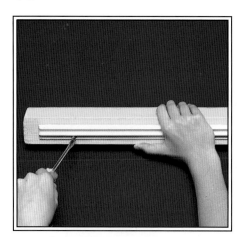

2 Ask an adult to saw the curtain rail to size if necessary. Place the track centrally on the wood and screw it into place. Screw in the end fittings at one end of the rail.

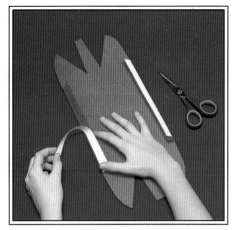

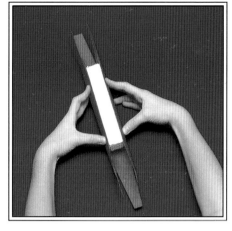

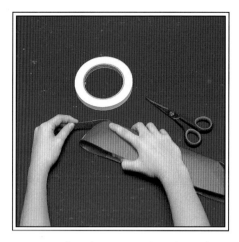

3 Copy the template on to the red card and cut it out. Score along the dotted lines and fold inwards. Stick double-sided tape along the outside of each folded section.

4 Remove the backing from the tape. Stick one side of the foam on to it. Fold the card over and press the other piece of double-sided tape to the opposite side of the foam.

5 Overlap the pointed ends at the back and front of the train and glue. Then glue the inside end of the top flaps, back and front. Fold them over and press firmly to secure.

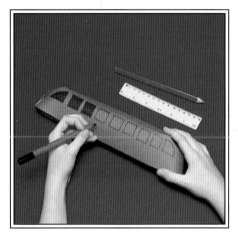

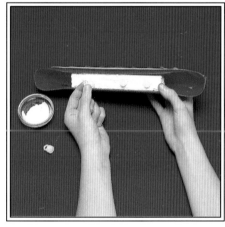

6 Pencil in windows along both sides of the train. Fill them in with a black felt tip pen. Paint decorative black and yellow stripes along the bottom of the windows.

7 Put a dab of glue on the 'eye' end of each plastic runner. Hold the train, foam bottom towards you. Push each runner in turn into the foam at roughly equal intervals.

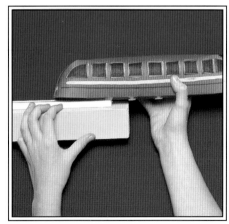

8 Stand the track on a flat surface. At the end of the track without an end stop, feed each plastic runner into the track. Run the train back and forth along the track.

The train you have made in this project is called a 'straddle' system monorail. Monorail trains running on the 'straddle' system rest on a single rail and are balanced and guided by side panels on either side of the train.

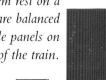
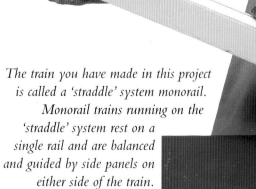

WORKING ON THE RAILWAYS

As the railways grew ever larger, so did the number of people employed to keep them running safely and on time. In Britain, for example, about 47,000 people worked for the railway companies by the late 1840s. Today, about 95,000 people are employed on the British railways – seven times less than during World War I (1914–18). One reason is that some jobs that were once done by people, such as selling tickets, are now done by machines. Automation has not been widespread, however. Most railways around the world have little money to buy computers and control systems.

Station-masters and train conductors are just some of the people who talk to passengers and deal with their needs. Most railway employees work behind the scenes, however, and rarely meet passengers. Managers plan how many trains should run on a particular line, how often and how fast. Engineering teams check and keep the tracks, signals and other equipment in safe working order.

Standing on the footplate
Two men worked in the driver's cab. They stood on the footplate because there were no seats. The driver was in charge. He managed the engine controls and the main brakes and kept a sharp look out for signals and anything blocking the track. The fireman stoked the fire and ensured the boiler contained enough water.

Laying track
Track workers check a section of track that has been newly laid with stone ballast, sleepers and rail. Rails should be checked regularly for cracks and deterioration. The ground beneath the rail can also subside and twist the rails.

Building trains
Workers in a factory are assembling an aluminium-bodied diesel train. Modern trains are built of either steel or aluminium sections welded together into a strong single unit. Separate units such as the driving cab, air-conditioning engine and toilets are fixed on the car later.

In the driving seat

Compared to the older steam engines, life is fairly comfortable in the cabs of modern locomotives. For a start, the driver can sit down. They are also protected from the weather inside fully enclosed cabs, and they do not have to stick their heads outside to see the track ahead. Today's drivers still manage the controls and brakes, and watch out for signals and obstacles on the track. They also have a lot of help from computerized railway systems.

FACT BOX
• There are more than 2,500 stations on Britain's mainline railways. Twenty of them are major terminals in London and other large cities.

• New York City's subway has more than 460 stations, London's Tube has 300 and Moscow's Metro about 150.

• Five people work on each World Heritage steam-powered locomotive on the Darjeeling–Himalaya Railway in India. As well as the driver, one man breaks the coal for the fireman. Two ride out front and sand the rails to stop the engine slipping on the steep slopes.

Insect debris

The windows of this train are being cleaned by hand, since this is the most effective way to remove the accumulation of flying insects on the cab windows. The bodies of most trains are cleaned in automatic washing plants using revolving brushes, high-pressure water jets and powerful cleaning agents that meet high environmental standards. In most cases, trains are cleaned every 24 hours when they come back to their home depot for examination and routine servicing.

Chefs on board

Armies of chefs and kitchen staff play an important role in making sure passengers do not go hungry during the journey. Most cooked food is prepared on board the train using microwave ovens and electric hobs. Almost all long-distance trains have dining and buffet cars, where passengers can take refreshment during their journeys. Even smaller trains often have buffet cars or mobile buffet trolleys.

DRESSED FOR THE JOB

MANY DIFFERENT railway workers began wearing special hats and uniforms during the 1840s, from train drivers to station-masters. A uniform makes the wearer look smart and efficient and lets him or her stand out in a crowd. This is essential if a passenger is looking for help in a busy train station. Uniforms are issued by the railway companies. Each company usually has its own special design for hat badges and uniform buttons.

In the past, different kinds of hat or badge often went with different jobs. The drivers of steam locomotives, for example, used to wear caps with shiny tops. Firemen were not issued with hats or uniforms. They wore overalls and often covered their heads with a knotted handkerchief. The first station-masters wore top hats instead of caps to show how important they were. When they later switched to caps, the brim was often decorated with gold braid, similar to the one you can make in this project.

Dressed for the job
A station-master and guard at Osaka Railway Station in Japan wear their distinctive dark uniforms, caps and sashes. The station-master, or area manager, has an extremely important role in running the railways. He or she is in charge of all aspects of running the station and must ensure that trains arrive and depart on time.

STATION-MASTER'S CAP

You will need: thin red card measuring 60 x 9cm, masking tape, thin red card measuring 11 x 11cm, scissors, thin red card measuring 26 x 15cm, pencil, sheet of white paper, pair of compasses, black felt, black paint, paintbrush, water pot, 40cm length of gold braid, extra card, gold paint.

1 Wrap the 60 x 9cm piece of red card around your head to get the right size. Then stick the two ends together with masking tape to make the circular crown of the hat.

2 Place the crown on the 11 x 11cm piece of red card. Hold the crown firmly and draw around it on to the flat piece of card. Cut out the circle to make the top of your hat.

3 Place the card circle on top of the crown of the hat. Join the two parts of the hat together using lots of strips of masking tape all the way around the join.

4 Place the hat over part of the 26 x 15cm piece of card. Draw a semi-circle by tracing around the hat edge. Start from one end of the semicircle, and draw a crescent shape as shown.

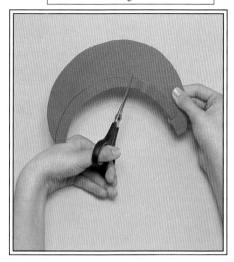

5 Use a pair of compasses to draw another semicircle 2cm in from the first. Cut out the crescent shape. Make cuts into the inner semicircle band all the way around to make tabs.

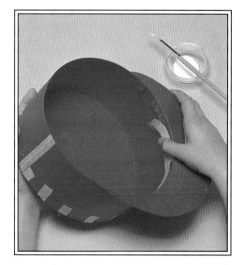

6 Fold the tabs up and glue around the edge of the crown where the peak will go. Fit the tabs inside the crown and stick them down. Cover the tabs with tape to hold firm.

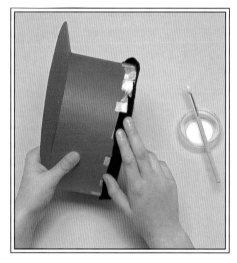

7 Place the hat, top down, on to a sheet of paper. Draw and cut out a circle 1cm wider than the hat. Pin it on the felt and cut out a felt circle. Glue this on to the top of the hat.

8 Cut a 60 x 10cm piece of felt. Glue this to the side of the hat, folding under at the bottom. At the peak, make a 2cm cut in the felt, and trim off the excess as shown.

9 Give the peak two coats of black paint. Let the paint dry between coats. Then glue on a piece of gold braid as shown above.

10 Design your own hat badge or copy the one shown in the picture. Draw it on a small piece of card and paint it gold. When the paint is dry, cut it out. Glue it to the front of the hat.

If you have a whistle, you could attach it to a piece of gold ribbon and hang it around your neck to complete the outfit.

TRAVELLING IN STYLE

First-class comforts
By the late 1800s, first-class passengers such as these elegantly dressed ladies enjoyed every comfort on their journey. There were soft, padded benches and armchairs and cloth-covered tea tables. The design of luxury railway carriages was based on that of top-class hotels. Windows had thick, plush curtains and fittings were made of polished wood and shiny brass.

IT WAS some time before travelling on a passenger train was as comfortable as waiting in one of the splendid stations. Before the 1850s, there were few luxuries and no toilets, even on long journeys. The overall comfort of the journey depended on how much money you had paid for your ticket. First-class carriages were – and still are – the most expensive and the most comfortable way to travel. Then came second class, third class and sometimes even fourth class.

The pioneer of comfortable rail travel was a US businessman called George Pullman. In 1859, after a particularly unpleasant train journey, he designed a coach in which "people could sleep and eat with more ease and comfort". Pullman launched his sleeping car in 1864, and was soon exporting luxury sleeping and dining carriages around the world.

Royal seal of approval
This luxurious railway carriage was made specially for Britain's Queen Victoria, who reigned from 1837 until her death in 1901. It had padded walls, thick carpets, expensive paintings on the walls and the finest decoration. Many European kings and queens had their own carriages built so that they could travel in royal style. Queen Victoria's carriage included a sleeping car, and it is thought she enjoyed sleeping in it more than at her palaces.

The Blue Train
South Africa's Blue Trains run between Cape Town and Pretoria in South Africa and are regarded as the most luxurious trains in the world. Passengers benefit from a 24-hour butler and laundry service and two lounge cars, and all the suites are equipped with televisions and telephones.

Lap of luxury

The *Orient-Express* first graced the railways of Europe in 1883. It formed a scheduled link between Paris, France, and Bucharest in Romania. The scheduled service stopped running in May 1977, and it was replaced by a new 'tourist-only' *Orient-Express* in May 1982. Passengers can once again enjoy the comfortable sleeping cars with velvet curtains, plush seats and five-course French cuisine in a Pullman dining carriage like the one shown above.

A rocky ride

The Canadian has a domed glass roof so that it offers spectacular views during the 4,467km journey from Toronto, on the east coast of Canada, to Vancouver, on the west. The journey lasts for three days and takes in the rolling prairies of Saskatchewan, Edmonton and Alberta. It then begins the gradual ascent through the foothills of the Rocky Mountains.

Lounging about

Long-distance trains on the Indian Pacific line from Sydney, on the Pacific Ocean, to Perth, on the Indian Ocean, are well equipped for the 65-hour journey across Australia. Indeed, they are described as being "luxury hotels on wheels". Passengers can relax and enjoy the entertainment provided in the comfortable surroundings of the train's lounge cars. These trains also have cafeterias, smart dining cars, club cars and two classes of accommodation. Passengers can eat, drink and sleep in comfort. The trains are even equipped with a honeymoon suite and a sick bay.

TRAINS ON FILM

WHEN THE French brothers Auguste and Louis Lumière showed one of their short films in 1895 of a train pulling into a station, many of the audience fled. They were terrified that the train would burst out of the screen into the room. Hardly anyone had ever seen a moving picture before, and people found them frighteningly realistic.

Trains have had a starring role in the movies ever since. The climax of many early movies, for example, involved the 'baddies' tying the heroine to a railway track, while the hero rushed to save her. Film-makers have continued to use trains to keep audiences on the edge of their seats. Nearly all the best train movies have been adventure thrillers.

In the early days, filming moving trains was a risky business. The cameras were bolted on the locomotive, while the camera operator leaned out or rode on a train on a parallel track. Such risks in filming would not be taken today.

Poetry, please
Night Mail (1936) showed scenes of mail being dropped off, and collected, by the 'Night Mail' train in Scotland. It was made to show postal workers how letters were carried on the mail train between England and Scotland. Later, the British born American poet W. H. Auden was asked to write verse for a voice-over. His poetry echoes the noises of the train as it made its long journey through the night.

Tears on the train
In the 1945 film *Brief Encounter,* two people (actors Trevor Howard and Celia Johnson) find romance in a railway station. Their love is doomed, however, as both are married. Much of the action was shot at Carnforth Station in Britain.

Railway children to the rescue
When a landslide threatens to derail a steam train in *The Railway Children* (1970), the children save the day by turning red petticoats into warning flags to signal to the driver. The film used old engines and coaches on a heritage railway in Yorkshire, Britain. It gives an insight into how steam trains and local stations operated in the early 1900s.

Smashing finish

A runaway train crashes through the walls of the station concourse in the thrilling climax to the 1976 action movie *Silver Streak*. Almost the whole movie is set on the train, during its two-and-a-half-day journey from Los Angeles to Chicago in the USA. Gene Wilder stars as the passenger who witnesses a murder on his first night and spends the rest of the journey battling off the baddies.

Bond on board

Roger Moore plays the smooth British agent in the 13th James Bond movie, *Octopussy* (released in 1983). Like all Bond movies, it is packed with breathtaking stunts and chases. During a gripping sequence on board a speeding train, Bond survives crawling below, along the sides and over the roof of the carriages. He also manages to jump off the train without getting hurt. Not something the rest of us should try! Sequences for the film were shot on real trains moving at low speeds. Stunt men were used for the most dangerous scenes.

Animal mischief

Indiana Jones and the Last Crusade (released in 1989) opens with a thrilling flashback. Young Indie is trying to escape pursuers by clambering along the top of a steam train. Chases are the stock-in-trade of adventure movies, but this one is different. The steam locomotive is hauling circus wagons. Indie falls into various cages, where he finds snakes, a rhinoceros and even a lion!

Race to the death

A speeding freight train carrying a stolen nuclear weapon is the setting for the nail-biting closing sequence of the 1996 action movie *Broken Arrow*. The hero (shown left, played by Christian Slater) scrambles over and under the freight wagons, as he attempts to wrest control of the train back from the villain (played by John Travolta) and disarm the bomb before it explodes.

RECORD BREAKERS

BIGGEST, FASTEST, steepest – trains and railways have been setting records ever since they were invented. Official speed records began when George and Robert Stephenson's *Rocket* reached a top speed of 48.3km/h in the 1829 Rainhill Trials. By the end of the 1800s, engineers were competing to produce a steam engine that could break the 100mph (161km/h) speed record.

Time-keeping was inaccurate until speedometers were fitted to locomotives during the 1900s. An American *No. 999* locomotive may have briefly managed 161km/h in 1893. The first steam trains capable of sustaining this kind of speed over long distances did not enter service until the 1930s.

World records are usually set over short distances, by locomotives hauling fewer carriages. When, for example, the 200mph (321.9km/h) barrier was broken in 1955 by two French Railways electric locomotives, each one was hauling just three carriages.

Claim to fame

The New York Central & Hudson River Railroad (NYC & HRR) built the 4-4-0 *No. 999* to haul its Empire State Express. On 11 May 1893, it was claimed that *No. 999* recorded a run of 181km/h between New York and Buffalo. The V-shaped 'cowcatcher' at the front was one of the distinctive features of American locomotives. Since great lengths of the American railroads were not fenced off, it was essential to protect the front of the locomotives from wandering animals such as buffalo. The cowcatcher performed this function very well.

Champion of steam

On 3 July 1938, Britain's A4-class Pacific *Mallard*'s sleek, streamlined bodywork helped it to set the world speed record for a steam locomotive. With driver Joe Duddington at the controls, backed up by fireman Tommy Bray, it reached 201km/h – a world steam record that remains unbeaten today. *Mallard* was designed by British engineer Sir Nigel Gresley. It remained in everyday service up until the early 1960s.

• The world's fastest regular passenger trains are the *Trains à Grande Vitesse* (TGV) on the French national services and the Eurostar trains linking London with Paris and Brussels in Belgium. Their maximum speed is 300km/h. The trains being built for Spanish Railways' new, high-speed, Madrid-to-Barcelona line will go even faster – 350km/h.

• The longest and heaviest freight train on record ran in West Virginia, USA, in 1967. The 500 coal wagons weighed 42,000 tonnes and stretched a distance of 6.5km.

• The world's longest passenger rail journey is on the Russian service between Moscow and Vladivostok. The 9,611km trip takes seven nights and crosses eight time zones.

Steep slopes

The *Pilatusbahn* in Lucerne, Switzerland, is the steepest rack-and-pinion railway in the world, climbing to a height of 2,070m above sea level. This system uses a rack laid between the rails. This links with a cog wheel under the engine as it drives the train up the steep 1:2 gradients (1m up for every 2m along).

Overcoming the obstacles

Mount Washington Railway in New Hampshire in the USA became the world's first mountain rack-and-pinion railway when it opened in 1869. At this time, mountain climbing and sightseeing by steam railway were great tourist attractions.

Shapes and sizes

1. Scotsman Patrick Stirling's Single locomotives, dating from 1870, are particularly striking locomotives. The driving wheels of these steam engines were a massive 2.5m in diameter.
2. The fastest electric trains are the French TGV (*Train à Grande Vitesse*). A modified TGV unit set the current world speed record of 515km/h.
3. By winning the Rainhill Trails in 1829, Robert and George Stephenson's *Rocket* put steam travel firmly on the world map, making this one of the most famous steam locomotives in the world.
4. The world's largest and most powerful steam engines are undoubtedly the Union Pacific Big Boys, each weighing over 500 tonnes.

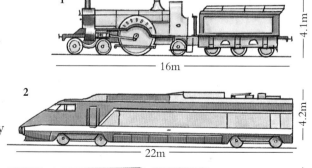

1

16m

4.1m

2

22m

4.2m

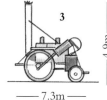

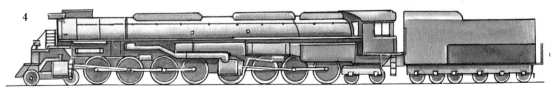

3

4.9m

7.3m

4

40.4m

5m

HIGH-SPEED TRAINS

THE RECORD-HOLDERS of today are the high-speed electric trains that whisk passengers between major city centres at 250–300km/h. These high-speed trains are the railway's answer to the competition from aeroplanes and motorways that grew up after World War II (1939–45). High-speed trains can travel at well over the legal limits for road traffic. Although they cannot travel as fast as planes, they save passengers time by taking them to city centres. In some cases, high-speed trains even beat the flying time between major cities such as London and Paris.

The world's first high-speed inter-city passenger service was launched in Japan on 1 October 1964. It linked the capital, Tokyo, with the major industrial city of Osaka in the south. The average speed of these trains – 220km/h – broke all the records for a passenger train service. The service was officially named the *Tokaido Shinkansen* (new high-speed railway), but its trains soon became known as Bullet Trains – because of their speed and the bullet-shaped noses of the locomotives.

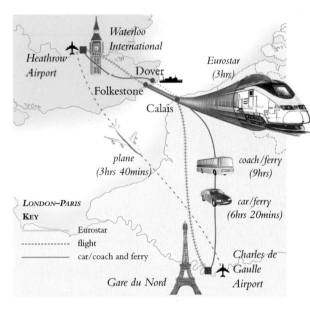

LONDON–PARIS KEY

Eurostar
---------- flight
———— car/coach and ferry

Market leader
The Eurostar has become the quickest way to travel between the city centres London, Britain, and Paris, France. It cuts out time-consuming airport check-in and transfer periods. Ferry crossings dramatically increase the journey times by car and by coach.

Rocket on rails
The latest high-speed JR500 trains to operate on Japan's *Tokaido Shinkansen* are as streamlined as a jetplane. Today, they can haul their 16 passenger carriages at 300km/h. The average speed of the trains in 1960 was 220km/h.

Stacking the odds

On some high-speed trains, such as this French TGV, passengers ride in double-decker carriages. The initials TGV are short for *Train à Grande Vitesse* (high-speed train). The operational speed of these French trains is 300km/h. TGVs also hold the current world speed record for a wheeled train. On 18 May 1990, a TGV Atlantique reached an amazing 515km/h.

Swedish tilter

The Swedish X2000 tilting electric trains have an average speed of 155km/h and a top speed of 200km/h. Tilting trains lean into curves to allow them to travel round bends at faster speeds than non-tilting trains.

Melting the ICE

Germany's ICE (InterCity Express) high-speed trains reached speeds of more than 400km/h during tests, before they entered service in 1992. Their maximum operating speed is about 280km/h. Like other high-speed trains, they are streamlined to reduce the slowing effects of drag.

Spanish speeders

Spain's elegant high-speed trains are called AVEs (*Alta Velocidad España*, or high speed of Spain). Their average operational speed is about 220km/h. They entered service on Spain's first high-speed railway, between Madrid and Seville, in 1992. The AVEs' design was based on the French TGVs. AVEs are made in France with some Spanish components. Like all high-speed trains, AVEs take their power from overhead electricity lines.

INVESTING IN THE FUTURE

To ACCELERATE to speeds of up to 300–350km/h, trains need to run on specially constructed tracks, with as few curves and slopes as possible. The tracks have to be wider apart than was usual in the past. A speeding train stirs the wind into eddies, which can buffet a passing train and jolt its passengers. The ride is also smoother and faster if continuously welded rails are used. If they have their own, dedicated lines, high-speed trains do not have to fit in with the timetables of ordinary, less speedy trains that would slow them down.

Throughout the world, railway companies are investing billions of pounds in building new lines or upgrading old track to carry their high-speed trains. In a few countries, people believe the future of land travel lies with an entirely different kind of train. Called maglevs, these trains 'fly' a few millimetres above their track, raised and propelled by magnetism.

Star performers
The Eurostar trains operate between England and Continental Europe. They can accelerate to 300km/h only when they reach the specially built, high-speed railway lines in France. The speed of the trains through southern England is limited because they run on normal track. Work on a new, British, high-speed line, the Channel Tunnel Rail Link between London St Pancras and Folkestone, is underway. It is expected to be completed in 2007 at a cost of more than £5.8 billion.

Scandinavian shuttle
These sleek, three-car, stainless-steel electric trains began running late in 1999 on a new railway built to link the centre of Oslo, the capital of Norway, with the new Gardermoen Airport, 48km to the north of the city. The maximum speed of these trains is 210km/h, which enables them to cover the journey in just over 19 minutes. The line includes Norway's longest railway tunnel at just under 14km.

Virgin express
Britain's Virgin Trains is investing a lot of money in new high-speed electric trains for its West Coast route between London and Glasgow. Work on upgrading old track to carry the trains is also underway. If all goes to plan, journey times between the two cities will be reduced from just over five hours in 1999 to just under four hours in 2005.

High-speed magnetism

Japanese maglev (short for magnetic levitation) trains have reached the astonishing speed of 552km/h on this specially constructed Yamanashi test line. This outstrips the world's fastest wheeled train, the TGV, by 39km/h. Maglevs are so speedy because they float above their track. They do not have wheels and they do not touch the rails. Rails solved the problem of the slowing force of friction between wheels and roads. Maglevs are the answer to reducing friction between wheels and rails.

Spanish AVE

Based on the design of the French TGV, the average operational speed of these trains is around 220km/h.

French TGV

A slightly modified TGV unit set the current world speed record for a train in a trial in 1990, reaching 515km/h.

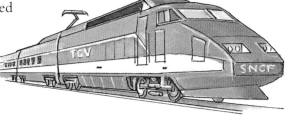

British Pendolino

A new generation of British high-speed tilting trains, designed to reach speeds of 220km/h.

German ICE

A former world speed record holder in 1988, reaching 404km/h. These trains entered into service in 1991.

Italian Pendolino

These trains run at speeds of around 250km/h on the existing network in Italy, tilting as they travel round curves.

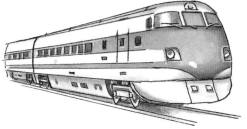

······· *High-speed lines – existing or under construction*

······· *Planned high-speed lines*

On the move in Europe

Many European railways are planning to develop high-speed rail networks over the next few years. One of the fastest routes will be the high-speed link between Madrid and Barcelona in Spain. The line will have some of the world's fastest passenger trains in service, running at speeds of up to 350km/h. By 2007, Spain will have 7,200km of high-speed rail networks with a fleet of over 280 trains.

By 2004 in France, tilting trains will cut around 30 minutes off the journey time between Paris and Toulouse. Some of the fastest short-distance trains are running in Norway between Oslo and Gardermoen Airport. They travel at up to 210km/h and cover 48km in just 19 minutes.

FLOATING TRAINS

MAGLEV (MAGNETICALLY levitated) trains need their own specially constructed tracks, called guideways, to move along. The trains are raised and propelled by powerful electromagnets. The special thing about magnets is that 'unlike' poles (north and south) attract each other or pull together, while 'like' poles (north and north, or south and south) repel or push apart. To make an electromagnet, an electric current flows through a wire or other conductor. When the direction of the current is changed, the magnetic poles switch, too.

A maglev train rises when one set of electromagnets beneath it repels another set in the guideway. The maglev is propelled by other electromagnets changing magnetic fields (switching poles). A set of electromagnets in the guideway ahead attracts electromagnets beneath the train, pulling it forward. As the train passes, the electromagnetic fields are switched. The maglev is repelled and pushed onwards to the next set of magnets on the guideway.

The main advantage of maglevs over normal wheeled trains is that they are faster because they are not slowed by friction. In tests in Germany in 1993, a maglev train reached speeds of 450km/h. Maglevs are also quieter and use less energy than wheeled trains.

Maglevs get moving
The technology behind maglevs was developed in the 1960s. The world's first service opened at Birmingham City Airport in Britain in the mid-1980s. Japan and Germany now lead the field in developing the technology. When the German Transrapid maglevs start running between Berlin and Hamburg in 2005, they will provide the world's first high-speed inter-city maglev service.

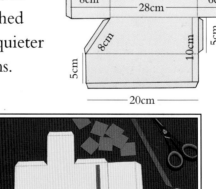

MODEL MAGLEV

You will need: *yellow card, pencil, ruler, scissors, red card, green card, glue and glue brush, blue card, double-sided sticky tape, 30 x 10cm wooden board, bradawl, two 8cm lengths thin dowel, wood glue, green and red paint, paintbrush, water pot, four magnets with holes in their centres.*

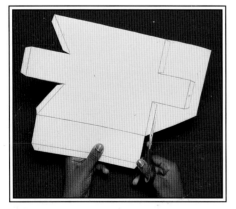

1 Copy the template on to a thin piece of yellow card. The tabs around the side of the template should be 1cm wide. Carefully cut around the outline.

2 Cut two strips of red card and glue them to each side of the template as shown. Cut the green card into window shapes and glue them to the front and sides.

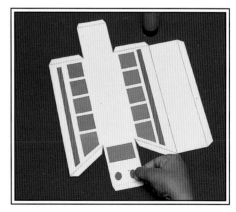

3 Continue to glue the windows to each side of the train to make two even rows. Cut two small blue card circles for headlights. Glue them to the front of the train as shown.

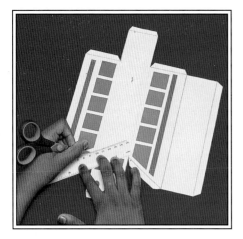

4 Leave the train template until the glue is completely dry. Then carefully use a pair of scissors and a ruler to score along the dotted lines for the tabs and the folds of the train.

5 Bend along the scored lines to form the basic shape of the train as shown above. Then cut small strips of double-sided sticky tape and stick them along each tab.

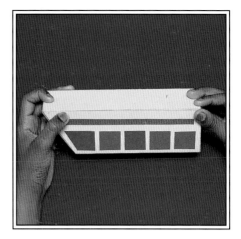

6 Stick the front and back sections of the train to the tabs on one side of the train. Repeat for the other side. Then stick the base section of the train to the opposite side.

7 Use a bradawl to pierce two holes in the wooden base, 9cm in from each end. Enlarge with a pencil. Put wood glue on the end of each piece of dowel and push one into each hole.

8 When the glue is dry give the base a coat of green paint. Paint two coats, letting the first dry before you apply the second. Then paint the dowel uprights a bright red.

9 Press the two magnets together so that they repel. These sides are the same poles – north or south. Use double-sided tape to fix the magnets to the base with like poles facing up.

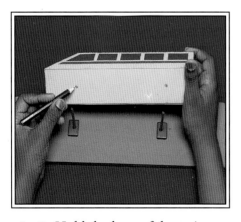

10 Hold the base of the train up to the dowel uprights. Mark two points in the centre of the base the same distance as between the uprights. Pierce through the marks.

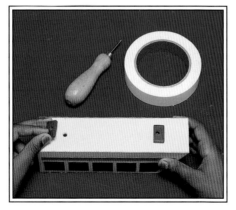

11 Push magnets over the dowel uprights to repel those on the base. Take them off and tape them over the holes in the train base so that these like poles face upwards.

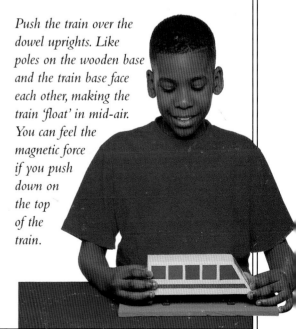

Push the train over the dowel uprights. Like poles on the wooden base and the train base face each other, making the train 'float' in mid-air. You can feel the magnetic force if you push down on the top of the train.

GLOSSARY

accelerator pedal
The pedal that controls the flow of fuel to a car engine.

air cooled
An engine in which the heat is carried away by air instead of water.

air pollution
The reduction of the oxygen content in the air with poisonous gases such as carbon monoxide.

airbag
A cushion stored in front of car seats that automatically inflates in a crash, protecting the driver and passengers.

all-terrain vehicles (ATVs)
Cars that are built for driving on rough surfaces.

Alta Velocidad Españã (AVE)
High-speed passenger trains that operate in Spain.

amphibious car
A car that travels on land and in water.

antilock braking systems (ABS)
A braking system that avoids wheels locking and skidding when the brakes are applied.

asphalt
A mixture of bitumen and concrete used to give roads a hard, smooth, weatherproof surface.

Automatic Train Protection (ATP)
A safety feature operating on some trains running on British railway networks. Trains pick up electronic signals from the track, which tell the driver to slow or stop the train. ATP automatically slows the train if the driver exceeds the speed limit.

Automatic Warning System (AWS)
A safety feature of all trains running on British railway networks. AWS informs the driver whether the track ahead is clear. Electric magnets between the rails send a message to the train, causing a bell to sound in the driver's cab if the track is clear. Otherwise, the magnet stays 'dead' and a horn sounds. AWS operates the brakes automatically if the driver does not respond to the signals.

ball bearing
A hardened steel ball, often arranged with other ball bearings around a turning surface to ease movement.

battery
A container of chemicals holding a charge of electricity.

bogie
A unit placed underneath a locomotive that guides the train around curves. The bogie also provides extra support for the locomotive. Four or six pivoted wheels are mounted on one bogie.

boiler
Part of a steam engine where steam is produced through the action of heat on water in the boiler tubes.

brake
A pad or disc that slows a moving surface down by pressing it.

brake van
A vehicle at the back of trains. A guard riding in the brake van applies the brakes on instruction from the driver in the locomotive at the front. This ensures that all of the carriages stay coupled.

bubble car
The name given to microcars such as the BMW Isetta, because of their round shape.

buffer
Rigid metal structure that absorbs the impact of a train to stop it at the end of the track.

Bullet Trains
The nickname of the high-speed, streamlined passenger trains that operate in Japan.

bumper
The protective, wraparound metal or rubber barrier that protects the front and rear of a car.

cabriolet
A car with a flexible roof that can be folded away into the rear of the car.

camshaft
A shaft, driven and timed with the engine crankshaft. Lobes rotate on the camshaft, opening and closing the valves in the cylinder head.

carbon monoxide
A poisonous gas that is a by-product of burning petrol.

carburettor
A unit that controls the fuel mixture entering the combustion chamber.

carriage
An individual compartment of a train that carries passengers – also known as a coach or car.

catenary
An overhead power cable supplying electricity to a train through a pantograph attached to the top of the locomotive.

chequered flag
A black-and-white flag that a race controller waves as a car crosses the finishing line.

chrome
A reflective metal used to cover car fittings such as bumpers and radiator grilles to make them look shiny.

classic car
A car that is collected and restored because of special qualities of design and workmanship.

coachwork
The outside body of a car.

conductor
The person responsible for the safety of passengers on a train. The conductor also checks and sometimes issues tickets.

container
A metal box that transports freight, making it easy to combine different methods of transportation.

convertible
A car that can be driven with and without a roof.

coupling
A connecting device that joins a locomotive to a carriage or wagon to make a train.

coupling rod
A link that connects the driving wheels on both sides of a locomotive. Coupling rods stop the wheels from slipping and even out the power distributed by the engine.

cowcatcher
A sloping, V-shaped plate attached to the front of American locomotives. It clears cattle and other obstructions from the line.

crankshaft
The part that transmits the four-stroke movement of the pistons to the car's driveline and road wheels.

custom car
A car that has been deliberately adapted by its owner to make it look and drive a certain way.

cut-and-cover construction
An early method of building underground tunnels. A large trench is cut into the earth along the line of the tunnel, lined with brick and then roofed over. Cut-and-cover construction has been eclipsed by the development of Tunnel-Boring Machines (TBMs).

cylinder
Hollow tube in which a piston moves.

dashboard
The vertical surface that contains the instruments facing a driver in a car.

drag racer
A car specially designed to take part in high-speed acceleration races.

driving wheel
The wheel of a locomotive that turns in response to power from the cylinder.

flange
A rim on the inside of the metal wheel of a locomotive that stops the wheels slipping sideways and falling off the rails.

flatbed
A small truck with a driver's cabin at the front and an open, horizontal platform at the rear.

Formula One
The class of racing car that has the most powerful engine specification.

four-wheel drive
A car in which power from the engine can be transferred to all four wheels, not just to the front or rear wheels.

freight
Goods transported by rail, road, sea or air.

friction
A force that stops or slows an object moving while it is in contact with another object.

fuel
A substance, such as petrol, that is burned to provide energy.

fuel efficient
A car that is designed to use as little fuel as possible while ensuring normal speed and power.

funicular
A railway that hauls one car up and one car down steep slopes.

gas
A non-solid, non-liquid substance given off when petrol burns. The name often used in the US for petrol.

gauge
The width between the inside running edges of the rails of a railway track.

gear
A toothed wheel designed to interact with other toothed wheels to transfer motion.

hot rod
A car in which the engine has been specially treated to allow it to accelerate rapidly and travel at high speed.

hump yard
An area beside a main rail route where freight wagons can be sorted. The wagons are pushed over the hump into sidings.

hydraulic
Worked by the pressure of fluid carried in pipes.

inner tube
A rubber tube filled with air, found inside the tyres of older vehicles.

InterCity Express (ICE)
The high-speed passenger trains that operate in Germany.

internal combustion
The burning of fuel in a closed chamber to generate power.

leading truck
The pair of leading wheels at the front of a locomotive.

limousine
Luxurious car featuring a glass partition behind the driver.

locomotive
An engine powered by steam, diesel or electricity and used to pull the carriages or wagons of a train.

lubrication
The smoothing of friction between parts of an engine, usually with oil.

maglev train
A high-speed train that is raised above a track and moves through the action of powerful electromagnets.

microcar
A particularly small car, designed for use in cities to minimize congestion.

monorail
A train that runs on a single rail.

motorway
Multi-lane road allowing traffic to travel long distances at speed.

mudguard
The wide wing of metal around a car wheel that prevents mud and stones from flying up off the road.

multi-purpose vehicle (MPV)
A car that has more than one use, for example, one that can carry as many passengers as a small van.

off-road vehicle (ORV)
A car that can drive on surfaces other than smooth, tarmac roads.

oil
A thick, black liquid found under the surface of the Earth from which petrol can be made.

oxygen
The gas that living creatures with lungs breathe.

pantograph
An assembly attached to the top of some locomotives that collects electricity from an overhead power supply. This electricity is then used to move the train.

pedestrian
A person who travels on foot.

pendolino
A train that tilts from side to side, enabling the train to move around curves at high speeds.

petrol
Liquid made from oil – the main fuel for internal combustion engines.

pickup
Truck with a cab at the front and a flat platform over the rear wheels.

piston
Device that moves within the cylinder. Each piston transforms steam pressure into wheel movement.

points
Rails on the track that guide the wheels of a locomotive on to a different section of track.

production line
A way of building machines in which the parts are added one by one in a continuous process.

prototype
The first attempt to build a working model from the design.

Pullman
A carriage where passengers can eat or sleep in luxurious surroundings.

rack-and-pinion railway
A railway that operates on steep slopes. A cogwheel engages its teeth on a rail that runs up the slope.

radiator
A container of water from which water is pumped around the engine.

recreational vehicle (RV)
A car designed for being driven on roads other than tarmac.

robot
A machine that is built to perform particular tasks automatically.

rolling stock
Vehicles that operate on a railway.

rubber
A liquid taken from rubber trees that forms a thick, flexible material suitable for making tyres.

seat belt
A safety strap worn by drivers and passengers to prevent injury in case of an accident.

signals
Messages transmitted to a locomotive to tell the train driver if the track ahead is clear. On modern trains, electronic signals are transmitted directly to the cabin.

sleeper
1. A horizontal concrete beam supporting the rails on a railway track. 2. A railway carriage providing sleeping accommodation for passengers.

speedometer
The dial on a dashboard that displays the speed at which a car is travelling.

sports car
An open or closed car built for performance, usually with two seats.

steam engine
An engine powered by the steam created by heating water.

steering mechanism
Combined system of steering wheel, rack and pinion mechanism and wheels that allows a driver to steer.

stock car
An ordinary car that has been adapted for racing.

straddle system
Monorails running on the straddle system rest on a single rail and are balanced and guided by side panels on either side of the train.

streamlining
Shaping a car's body so that it can travel with low air resistance.

suspension system
The springs and shock absorbers that cushion the movement of a car's wheels on the road.

train
A number of passenger carriages or freight wagons coupled together. Trains can be self-propelled or hauled by a locomotive.

***Train à Grande Vitesse* (TGV)**
The name of the high-speed, streamlined passenger trains that operate in France.

Train Protection and Warning System (TPWS)
An improved version of the British safety feature AWS. TPWS uses existing AWS safety measures but also incorporates an automatic stop at a red signal and a speed trap in advance of the signal.

Tunnel-Boring Machine (TBM)
A digging device that grinds through soft rock, such as chalk, using a giant, rotating, cutting head.

veteran car
Any car built before 1905.

vintage car
Any car built between 1919 and 1930.

wind tunnel
A large chamber in which powerful draughts of air are blown over a car to test and measure how much air resistance the car shows.

INDEX

ACKNOWLEDGEMENTS

The publishers would like to thank the following children, and their parents, for modelling in this book: Tyrone Agiton, Katie Appleby, Erin Bhogal, Joseph Brightman, Shaun Liam Cook, Stacie Damps, Brooke Griffiths, Thomas James, Eddie Lengthorn, Gabrielle Locke, Emma Molley, Nicky Payne, Jamie Pyle, Zoe Richardson, Ajvir Sandhu, Jasmine Sharland and Amber-Hollie Wood.

PICTURE CREDITS Advertising Archive: 44tl; All Sport: 23tr, 23tl, 23cr, 23b, 25bl, 30b, 30b; Agence Vandystadt: 23cr; Alvey and Towers Picture Library: 84cl, 93tl, 103t, 103cl, 103br, 111c, 117br; Art Archive: 11tr, 40bl; The Bridgeman Art Library: 22c; Colin Boocock: 87br; Corbis/Morton Beebe, S.F.: 117t; Corbis/Bettmann: 89cl; Corbis/Dallas and John Heaton: 116b; Corbis/John Heseltine: 85bl; Corbis/Jeremy Horner: 96tl; Corbis/Hulton Getty: 102cl; Corbis/Wolfgang Kaehler: 111b; Corbis/Lake County Museum: 67t; Corbis/Milepost 92½: 99tl; Corbis/Paul A. Souders: 87tl; Corbis/Michael S. Yamashita: 89cr, 94b, 108tr; Chris Dixon: i, 118br; EON Productions: 33tl; Genesis: 28bl; Ronald Grant Archive: 21cr, 33tr, 47tr, 57t, 63b; Mike Harris: 117cr, 118bl; Hulton Getty: 18tr; Anthony J. Lambert Collection: front cover (br), 66t, 83tr, 85br, 110tl, 115tl; *The Illustrated London News:* 100t, 100br, 110bl; Image Bank: 28tl, 38bl, 44c; Jaguar: 46tr, 47bl; The Kobal Collection: 57bl, 112bl, 112br, 113tl, 113tr, 113bl, 113br, 123bl; LAT: 22bl, 54b, 55bl; London Underground Ltd: 77cr; Mary Evans Picture Library: 74b, 76t, 77t, 77cl, 78t, 78b, 82t, 82c, 84tl, 88tr, 88b, 98cr, 98bl, 102br; Milepost 92½: front cover (cl), back cover (cl), 4b, 64–65, 66c, 67cl, 67cr, 68t, 70b, 71bl, 73br, 74t, 75cl, 75cr, 79c, 79b, 80t, 82b, 83tl, 83cr, 83b, 84cr, 85t, 86t, 86b, 87tr, 87bl, 89b, 93tl, 95t, 95cr, 99cl, 99br, 101tl, 101cl, 104tr, 106bl, 106br, 107t, 107c, 107b, 110br, 112tr, 117cl, 118t, 119tl, 124tr; Millbrook House Ltd: 88c, 90tl; Don Morley: 9cr, 14tr, 14bl, 17tl, 21tl, 26bl, 27tl, 27tr, 27cr, 27 br, 28cr, 29tr, 30t, 48tr, 54tl, 55br, 55c, 55tr, 56b, 61cr; Brian Morrison: 75b, 123tr; National Motor Museum: 8br, 29br, 32t, 32b, 40cr, 41cr, 45tl, 47tl, 51cl, 56t, 56c, 57cr, 62br, 63cl; PA News Photo Library: 32bl, 32br; QA Photos Ltd: 101cr; Quadrant: 4tr, 5tl, 8tr, 8bl, 9tr, 9cl, 9bl, 9tl, 14cl, 15c, 16br, 17br, 21tr, 26br, 26tl, 27cl, 27bl, 29bl, 30cr, 34tl, 37tr, 37cl, 42tr, 44bl, 45tr, 46br, 48cl, 49tl, 49cl, 49br, 50tl, 51cr, 51b, 52cr, 57br, 58bl, 58br, 61bl, 125t; Claire Rae: 115cr; Rail Images: front jacket flap; RAWIE: 95bl, 95bc; Science and Society/National Railway Museum: 70t, 98t, 114b, 120t; Science and Society/London Transport Museum: 102tl; Smart Car: 62tl, 62tr; SNCF-CAV/Sylvain Cambon: 77b; SNCF-CAV/Jean-Marc Fabbro: 92b; Tony Stone: 14tl, 20bl, 29tl, 29c, 36tl, 36bl, 37tl, 37bl, 37br, 38br, 40cr, 41tr, 41b, 46bl, 51tl, 52tl, 52bl, 58tl, 59tr, 59c, 126bl; Sutton Motorsport Images: front cover (c); Volkswagen Press: 49tr.

Every effort has been made to trace the copyright holders of all images that appear in this book. Anness Publishing Ltd apologises for any unintentional omissions and, if notified, would be happy to add an acknowledgement in future editions.